THE ROUND DANCE OF THE STARS

THE ROUND DANCE OF THE STARS

Poems by

Daniel Orsini

Quaternity™

THE ROUND DANCE OF THE STARS

Quaternity Books™
Copyright © 2023 by Daniel Orsini
First Edition Quaternity™ Books
ISBN – 978-1-943691-36-4
Cover Design by James Buchanan

The first man was made 'of the dust of the earth'; the second man is from heaven. The man made of dust is the pattern of all men of dust, and the heavenly man is the pattern of all the heavenly. As we have worn the likeness of the man made of dust, so we shall wear the likeness of the heavenly man.

—1 Corinthians 15.47-49

Those are called gods to whom the word of God was delivered—and Scripture cannot be set aside.

—John 10.35

CONTENTS

Introduction   9

Bootstrap	17	Light of the Eye	41
Cat's Eye	18	Local Bubble	42
Chain-Linked	19	The Man in the Moon	43
Channeling Hipparchus	20	Mastermind	44
The Chariot of Aristotle's Wheels	21	A Methane Snow	45
Christ on Einstein's Tram	22	The Moon in Transition Raised to the Sun	46
Circumambient	23	The Path of Least Action	47
Claim	24	Psalter	48
Containment and the Cosmic Edge	25	Rebis	49
Cosmic Dust	26	Rite	50
Courtship	27	The Round Dance of the Stars	51
The Cusp of Skill	28	Schrödinger's Cat	52
Drilling on Mars	29	Scintilla's Scan	53
Ephesian Symbols	30	Scion	54
Evangelist	31	Scout	55
Extract of the Macrocosm	32	The Smoke-Hole of the Tent	56
Fabricator	33	Spacetime's Wight	57
Fixated on Mars	34	The Spear of Archytas	58
Gatekeeper	35	Splitting the Earth with a Straight Foot	59
Gateway	36	Storyboard	60
The Heavenly Journey of the Shaman	37	Trapeze	61
Here Be Dragons	38	The Water That Does Not Make the Hands Wet	62
A Host-Star in Draco	39	Waxing in Luna into the Nature of the Sun	63
The Jesus of Psychoanalysis	40	The Woman in the Moon	64

Notes and Comments   65

THE ROUND DANCE OF THE STARS
INTRODUCTION
Daniel Orsini

In "Circles," perhaps his most "far-shining"[1] moral essay, Ralph Waldo Emerson reminds us that "St. Augustine described the nature of God as a circle whose centre was everywhere and its circumference nowhere."[2] Subsequently, as Emerson himself "sweeps serenely over God's depths into an infinite sea,"[3] he remarks that "There is no outside, no inclosing wall, no circumference to us."[4] In other words, each individual extends the outline of his own sphere of being.

However, throughout *The Round Dance of the Stars,* even as he advocates Emerson's position, the "awakened"[5] speaker also underscores a key Jungian idea: "the anthropoid—man as an archaic fact—[must] be put together again."[6] Not surprisingly, then, in "Trapeze," alert to both Jung's ancestral "play of apes" and the hallowed warmth of self-incubation, the phantom biped seeks "The foetus in the room" (line 8), the astrological Christ-figure who, in "Waxing in Luna into the Nature of the Sun," is also the spagyric foetus—the storied embryo of the divine child. In alchemy, the word *spagyric* refers to a process that both separates and combines.[7] Simply put, the spagyric foetus ascends into heaven that it may become a spirit from a body and then descends to earth that it may become a body again. In effect, the spagyric birth "is nothing other than the *filius philosophorum,* the inner, eternal man in the shell of the outer, mortal man."[8]

Still, here, a seeming contradiction occurs—according to Saint John the Apostle, "'No one ever went up to heaven except the one who came down from heaven, the Son of Man whose home is in heaven'" (3.13).[9] Indeed, Jung himself suggests that this—the hypostatic "union of the wholly divine nature and of a wholly human nature in the one person of Jesus Christ" ("Hypostasis" [n.], def. 4c)[10]—remains a quandary no less than a conundrum that the Church has never fully resolved, mainly because transformational religious concepts often prove as circuitous as they are ineffable. Broadly speaking, dogmas are approximate concepts for a fact that exists yet cannot be described and therefore can only be approached by circumambulation.[11]

Nevertheless, in the context of *this* essay, both the "quandary" and the "conundrum" of the hypostatic union have long since been resolved, since Christ has already been "manifested in the body, / vindicated in the spirit, / seen by angels, [. . .] proclaimed among the nations, believed in throughout the world, [and] glorified in high heaven," as Saint Paul attests in The Second Letter to Timothy (3.16). In effect, through both the Incarnation and the hypostatic union, Christ became a *theoanthropic* Person—true God and true man—with distinct and unmixed divine and human attributes, in order that, thereafter, having witnessed the power of the Holy Spirit [the Innermost Self of the Father and the Son], Christ might tabernacle each and every twice-born believer in the Word. In fact, according to Andrew Murray, "Before Christ, spiritual life was external and preparatory. The indwelling of the Spirit was unknown" because the human subject "had not yet become a temple of God in the Spirit."[12] However, eventually, the Father "sent the Spirit of His Son, the Spirit of Christ, to be in us," that we might become "partakers of the divine nature" in the continuation of our own Pentecost.[13] Moreover, that such an "actual presence" is approachable now through circumambulation—i.e., through the centering power of the archetypal symbol: "a holiest of All in that temple which we are"[14]—may well be inarguable.

Thus, in "Splitting the Earth with a Straight Foot," one of the key poems in this collection, the speaker characterizes himself as a spiritual body, the transcendental self that, being posited, tabernacled, and indwelt by God, is "Circumambient, like His cosmic eye" (1). With these loaded words, the speaker, echoing Jung, emphasizes not only that the "soul of the substances" is spherical,[15] but also that, "like every archetype, the self cannot be localized in an individual ego-consciousness, but acts like a circumambient [or surrounding] atmosphere to which no limits can be set, either in space or in time."[16]

Equally revealing is the link between circle and quaternity as "activated archetypes"[17] in "The Chariot of Aristotle's Wheels." In the latter poem, the speaker offers Jung's hypothetical description of the alchemical *opus* as a chariot, both a spherical vessel[18] and a value-concept[19] derived from Aristotle's wheel symbolism. Jung proposes that the totality of the numinous self "appears in quaternary form only when it is not just an unconscious fact but a conscious and differentiated totality; for instance, when the horizon is thought of not simply as a circle but as consisting of four clearly defined points." Jung explains that, psychologically, "The quaternity of basic functions of consciousness [thinking, feeling, sensing, and intuiting] meets this requirement." Accordingly, "one's given personality could be represented by a continuous circle," whereas the conscious personality would be "a circle that can be divided into any number of parts but as consisting of four clearly defined points." Furthermore, since "It is only to be expected that the chariot should have four wheels to correspond with the four elements or natures" as a symbol of wholeness, the circle by itself is "a defective quaternity." By contrast, "The chariot as a spherical vessel and as consciousness rests on the four elements or basic functions, just as the floating island where Apollo was born, Delos, rested on the four supports which Poseidon made for it. The wheels, naturally, are on the outside of the chariot and are its motor organs, just as the functions of consciousness facilitate the relation of the psyche to its environment. [. . .] The 'chariot of Aristotle'[20] [. . .] can be understood in this sense as a symbol of the [discriminated] self."[21]

Clearly, for Jung, the character of the "realized"[22] Self is "antinomial."[23] Hence, in "Chain-Linked" the Christ-centered astronaut is "Both round and square" (16). With this image alone, the speaker, set free "from sin as a power,"[24] echoes the "stammering utterance"[25] that the soul is "round"[26] even as he refers, with equal emphasis, to "the four quarters of the world"[27] and hence not only to Christ, the quadripartite "unitary being who existed before man" and who represents "man's wholeness," but also to "the unity of the Spirit [of Christ]" that exists within the undivided believer himself.[28] In fact, in "The Heavenly Journey of the Shaman," prodded at first unconsciously,[29] through the archetypes, to holistic self-enlightenment and then consciously, in "the tension of opposites,"[30] to even sharper discrimination, the speaker responds to a recurrent embodiment of the God-image: the NASA astronaut himself portrayed as coheir of Christ, but with a surprising twist—the lacerating image of the "Cross-beams' quaternity" (18), i.e., "the quaternity of Christ [. . .] exemplified by the cross symbol."[31] In effect, the [suffering] inhabitant of the quadratic space leads to the rounded human figure, in Jung's view the commonest symbol of the [Christ-centered] self. Thus, the spiritual seeker in "Storyboard" proclaims that "Within the four quarters I sought to roam / Infinity's circle" (21-22). Likewise, in "Extract of the Macrocosm," the speaker alludes to "Chiliasm's Four," i.e., not only to the belief in the coming of the promised millennium, but also to an image of the total self, a psychologically quadratic figure not unlike "the squared circle" of the crucified Christ,[32] the latter icon, in Jungian texts, a symbol of conscious discrimination.

Of course, in *The Round Dance of the Stars,* perhaps the exalted status accorded the believer-priest is most evident in the title poem. Jung himself explicates the related concept of the squared circle, and hence the "mystical 'round dance' which Christ instituted before [H[is crucifixion," in *Psychology and Western Religion:* "Since olden times the circle with a centre has been a symbol for the Deity, illustrating the wholeness of God incarnate: the single point in the centre and the series of points constituting the circumference." Almost inevitably, then, "Ritual circumambulation often bases itself quite consciously on the cosmic picture of the starry heavens revolving, [i.e.,] on the 'dance of the stars,' an idea that is still preserved in the comparison of the twelve disciples with the zodiacal constellations, [and] also in the depictions of the zodiac that are sometimes found in churches, in front of the altar or on the roof of the nave. [. . .] At all events, the aim and effect of the solemn round dance is to impress upon the mind the image of the circle and the centre [Christ] and the relation of each point along the periphery to that centre. Psychologically this arrangement is equivalent to a mandala and is thus a symbol of the [quadratic] self, the point of reference not only of the individual ego but of all those who are of like mind or who are bound together by fate."[33]

After the "indwelling Spirit"[34] speaks, what else is there to say? Throughout *The Round Dance of the Stars,* since "Natural man is not a self,"[35] and since the totality of the self "transcends our vision,"[36] and, too, since "All the souls of the world [are] contained in Him" ("Containment and the Cosmic Edge" 24), The Mystical Body of Christ—His united, Pentecostal Church—may well become the *inspired* shared goal of wayfarers, spacewalkers, and saints alike, with each "round dancer" not an illusory reality, but rather "the [self-realized] universal and everlasting man as distinct from the ephemeral and 'accidental' mortal man"[37]—in fine, the Christ-centered being who exists both *in* time and *beyond* time.

Cranston, Rhode Island
27 May 2023

ENDNOTES

[1] Cf. Andrew J. George, "Biographical Note," in *Essays by Ralph Waldo Emerson,* introd. Irwin Erdman (1926; New York: Harper, 1951) xxiv: "humanity began to see in him [Emerson] one of the far-shining children of men."

[2] See *Essays by Ralph Waldo Emerson* 212.

[3] This is an interpolated quote from "Spiritual Laws," in *Essays by Ralph Waldo Emerson* 100.

[4] The source is "Circles," in *Essays by Ralph Waldo Emerson* 215.

[5] This epithet evokes but the outline of the sphere of the Spirit-quickened speaker from "The Oversoul," in *Essays by Ralph Waldo Emerson* 197-98: "The soul is the perceiver and revealer of truth. We know truth when we see it, let sceptic and scoffer say what they choose. Foolish people ask you, when you have spoken what they do not wish to hear, 'How do you know it is truth, and not an error of your own?' We know truth when we see it, from opinion, as we know when we are awake that we are awake."

[6] C. G. Jung explores this "Dionysian mystery," a play of apes that leads "down into natural history, into the bestial instinctive foundations of human existence," in *Psychology and Alchemy,* trans. R. F. C. Hull (1953; Princeton: Princeton UP, 1993) 129, 131. According to Jung, these "rites of renewal" are "attempts to abolish the separation between the conscious mind and the unconscious, the real source of life, and to bring about a reunion of the individual with the native soil of his inherited, instinctive make-up" (137). In my essay, I focus on another aspect of the "mystery": "the Spirit of Christ" within us that "equips us for acceptable worship" as empowered witnesses to the *personal* Jesus (Andrew Murray, *The Spirit of Christ* [Pennsylvania: Whitaker House, n.d.] 60, 71) and is a gift of the Holy Ghost. See also "Claim," a key poem in *The Round Dance of the Stars,* where the speaker—having tracked the quaternity of the totalistic self, i.e., the supreme and essential synthesis of male and female—"From anthropoid to hierophant [. . .] reconstructed an archaic fact" (lines 7-8).

[7] C. G. Jung defines "the root of the word 'spagyric'" in *Mysterium Coniunctionis: An Inquiry into the Separation and Synthesis of Psychic Opposites in Alchemy,* trans. R. F. C. Hull (1963; Princeton: Princeton UP, 1977) 481n91: "to rend, tear, stretch out" and "to bring or collect together."

[8] C. G. Jung, *Alchemical Studies,* trans. R. F. C. Hull (1967; Princeton: Princeton UP, 1976) 150.

[9] The citation is from *The New English Bible with the Apocrypha* (1961; New York: Oxford UP, 1972), an ecumenical text.

[10] See *Webster's New World Dictionary,* 1988 ed.

[11] Jung, *Mysterium Coniunctionis* 102-03n54. Of course, here, despite its power as a transpersonal symbol of spiritual rebirth, the redeemer-figure of alchemy "is not commensurable with Christ. Whereas Christ is God and is begotten by the Father" (104), the spagyric foetus is no more than the offspring of a wind-god, a material earth-spirit that, according to Jung, "behaves in an all too Basilidian [i.e., Gnostic] manner, [but] with a Christian alibi" (221). However, elsewhere, Jung suggests that "the identification or paralleling of Christ" with the spagyric foetus (126), like the alchemist's "antique feeling for nature," does not yield "only a reductive meaning, but one that is prospective and spiritual. [. . .] The more serious alchemists, if we are to believe their statements, were religious people who had no thought of criticizing religious truth. There is in the literature of alchemy, so far

as I can judge, no attack on dogma. [. . .] Not only were the old Masters not critical of ecclesiastical doctrine, they were, on the contrary, convinced that their discoveries, real or imaginary, would enrich the doctrine of the correspondence of heavenly and earthly things, since they endeavoured to prove that the 'mystery of faith' was reflected in the world of nature" (309-10). In short, "although the alchemists failed to discover the hidden structure of matter, they did discover that of the psyche, even if they were scarcely conscious of what this discovery meant"—specifically, that, "in the psyche's secret and quite irrational participation in its own mysterium," hallowed religious beliefs "have, besides their supernatural foundation, a basis in psychological facts whose existence is as valid as those of the empirical sciences" (126-27, 153n317).

[12] Murray, *The Spirit of Christ* 90.

[13] Murray, *The Spirit of Christ* 70-71. See also John 10.35: "Those are called gods to whom the word of God was delivered—and Scripture cannot be set aside."

[14] Murray, *The Spirit of Christ* 210.

[15] Jung remarks that "The thinking in the Psalms and of the prophets is [also] circular" and that "Even the Apocalypse consists of spiral images." In fact, "One of the main characteristics of Gnostic thinking is circularity" (*Mysterium Coniunctionis* 102-03n54). See also *Psychology and Alchemy* 84n38, where Jung mentions "the spherical form of Plato's Original Man."

[16] C. G. Jung clarifies this assertion in *Aion: Researches into the Phenomenology of the Self*, trans. R. F. C. Hull (1959; Princeton: Princeton UP, 1978) 167-71: "For the alchemist it was clear that the 'centre,' or what we would call the self, does not lie in the ego but is outside it, 'in us' yet not 'in our mind,' being located rather in that which we unconsciously are, the 'quid' [the 'what,' the neutral self] which we still have to recognize. Today we would call it the unconscious, and we distinguish between a personal unconscious which enables us to recognize the shadow and an impersonal unconscious which enables us to recognize the archetypal symbol of the self. Such a point of view was inaccessible to the alchemist [here, Gerhard Dorn (c. 1530-1584)], and having no idea of the theory of knowledge, he had to exteriorize his archetype in the traditional way and lodge it in matter [the living philosophical stone], even though he felt [. . .] that the centre was paradoxically in man and yet at the same time outside him" and that, everywhere, it came, "like his own [centre], from the same fountainhead," i.e., "'the image of God which in us.'"

[17] Jung, *Aion* 168.

[18] Jung refers to the chariot as a spherical vessel in *Mysterium Coniunctionis* 203.

[19] Jung underscores "the moral as well as the energic value of the conscious and the unconscious personality" in *Mysterium Coniunctionis* 427.

[20] This symbol surfaces in an alchemical recipe "Written of old and gathered together by a certain Christian Philosopher" in the "Tractat[ul]us Aristotelis ad Alexandrum Magnum" (*Mysterium Coniunctionis* 201-02n478).

[21] Jung, *Mysterium Coniunctionis* 203.

[22] According to Jung, "the realization of the self," which is "not just an intellectual act but is primarily a moral one," may lead the individual to the "development of consciousness" (*Alchemical Studies* 264). However, "redemption depends" on more than the compliant "imitation" of Christ; crucially, it depends "on the work" that the faith-based disciple "does on himself." Since "Moral unmasking is but a step further in the same direction," and since thereafter, not without the gravest struggle, he recognizes "man as he is, [. . .] if he knows

the significance of what he is doing, he could belong to a higher order of man who makes real the Christ symbol, regardless of the suffering involved." In fact, "it might easily happen to contemporary man [. . .] that the person Jesus, now existing outside in the realm of history, might become the higher man within himself. Then we would have attained, in a European way, the psychological state corresponding to Eastern enlightenment." Of course, it should not be surprising that Jung prefers a "psychological" rather than a "metaphysical" interpretation of Murray's "Baptism of the Spirit." Even so, for Jung, "higher consciousness" is "real, a reality we can do something with, a living reality full of possibilities" (54).

[23] Jung asserts that the character of the self is "antinomial," i.e., "both conflict and unity," in *Psychology and Alchemy* 21.

[24] Murray, *The Spirit of Christ* 143.

[25] Murray, *The Spirit of Christ* 170.

[26] Jung, *Mysterium Coniunctionis* 140.

[27] Jung, *Psychology and Alchemy* 132.

[28] Murray, *The Spirit of Christ* 234.

[29] Jung, *Alchemical Studies* 254-55.

[30] Jung, *Alchemical Studies* 243.

[31] Jung, *Aion* 204.

[32] Jung, *Aion* 204. See also *Mysterium Coniunctionis* 347, where Jung extols his beloved archetypes as transpersonal patterns of thought: "Life wants to create new forms, and therefore [. . .] it must perforce activate the archetype that has always helped man to express the mystery of the soul. [. . .] I maintain that the psychic archetype [here, the squared circle of the self] makes it possible for the divine figure to take form and become accessible to understanding."

[33] Jung reminds us that, in the Acts of John, "one of the most important of the apocryphal texts that have come down to us," Christ "told his disciples to hold hands and form a ring, while he himself stood in the centre. As they moved round in a circle, Christ sang a song of praise" that included the following pertinent verses: "'The Twelve paces the round aloft, Amen. / To each and all it is given to dance, Amen'" (169-70, 172).

[34] Murray, *The Spirit of Christ* 158 and 11: "The Holy Spirit is the Spirit of the holy life which was and is in Christ Jesus, and which works in us as a divine life-power. He is the Spirit of holiness, and only as such will He lead us. God works in us both to will and to do His good pleasure through Him. God made us perfect in every good work to do His will through the Spirit's working in us that which is pleasing in His sight. To be led of the Spirit implies the surrender to His work as He convicts of sin and cleanses soul and body for His temple. It is the [new] indwelling [Holy] Spirit, filling, sanctifying, and ruling the heart and life, that He [the Innermost Self of the Father and the Son] enlightens and leads."

[35] Jung, *Psychology and Alchemy* 81.

[36] Jung, *Psychology and Alchemy* 182.

[37] Jung, *Psychology and Alchemy* 48.

THE ROUND DANCE OF THE STARS

DANIEL ORSINI

BOOTSTRAP

Attached to our bodies, their pathways set—

A maze of fibers: clusters dry or wet

Or coiled in the sunbeam or spread like sweat—

Our brain cells vacillate lest we forget.

From stone to touch, receptors slot the skin

Like loops that intersect. — Hub in the tin,

The cortex shambles; modifies its spin;

While Robonaut bobbles, bootstraps the din.

He fabricates the contents of the scene:

Capsules, depths, and crescents; bulk like a bean;

Vault above the terebinths; slopes that preen;

Spirit in the cirri, semblance or screen.

The eye of the peacock ruled by its ray,

Son of Man standing, should hybrids yet bray,

Plumules that scatter, coverts that decay

Shall wash their dots and then witness the day.

Reality before us, nets that flow

Evoke from each captive treasures that grow

Both tall and thin, like Einstein's tram, so slow

We twine such skein as senses overthrow.

Even as Hermes in his capsule curled,

Elastic its weave, by the magus twirled,

He enters the holon: tesseract purled,

Hyperspace infinite, hyphenate furled.

CAT'S EYE

The Spindle Galaxy, with disks like dust,
Floats in the chaos; spagyric as rust,
A Spiral with a tail, colliding, thrust,
Wriggles across space, as the Tadpole must.
Heaven yet surges. — Like Heracles' car,
Or Hermes' syrinx from Pandora's jar,
The Cat's Eye Nebula, where light years are,
Layers its shells around a dying star.

I think of days that, like numbers, recede;
That sleep may pare or Eternity feed.
Product of the opus, *filius,* seed
Coterminous with God, His sweat or His bead,
Suspended He hangs: the Child in the drum—
Stumbling Stone or Scion—He is the sum.
Tall as a dactyl, tiny as a thumb,
Like gum with gum, we are what we become.

The Big Bang had passed; then titanic, clear,
The first star formed and then copies that peer
Either at His birth or else at His bier.
But how could they know that He would be here?
Hospitable to life, from nothing spun—
In its mound—the collarbone of the One;
A sacred fig tree; as white as the Sun,
A thousand gemstones on Möbius' run.

CHAIN-LINKED

Because the conflagration is not done,
That we may save the world, we work as One;
Undock at the station that we have spun;
Deploy five CubeSats on Möbius' run.
We enter the subset as through a door;
Made in the image of an image store
Palm trees and terebinths; bulk at the core;
In the omniverse, astronauts that pour.

I searched a face as dominant as Shem
Dressed like the sun; the *rebis* in the REM
Without an ego, Cartesian its stem—
The fulfillment of Ge's mythologem.
In the midst of Chaos I tipped the cone;
Assembled all my souls; discerned the clone;
Heard through my earphone the mystagog moan;
Both round and square, traversed the zone alone.

I shifted my shape to cradle its stress.
That all its molecules might coalesce,
I clasped its skin; colossal its caress,
Controlled its coil; mechatronic my press,
Maneuvered my unit; heedless of harm—
Skein of Hephaestus—chain-linked my alarm
Even as matter; manifested charm;
Grappled Hubble with my robotic arm.

CHANNELING HIPPARCHUS

As I twine my skein, its ball having spun
In my inmost eye, the Milky Way won,
A strand continues that I cannot shun,
Its rim, not its hub, outrun by the Sun.
Still I track Polaris. Stars like débris
Abound on my plate till clusters that flee—
Scions in their arms—evolve like a plea,
Then imbed in dust of the nebulae.

I look down first and then farther away;
Examine ancient light; impeach its ray,
Kilometers measured in its delay
Disturbed as strata or, postponed, the day.
Channeling Hipparchus, I take a risk—
Joined with Atlas, I commandeer each disk,
Like tori that curve or cuboids that whisk,
Totality brisk as an asterisk.

Solemn now I go where the action is;
Search the Sun's magnetic field; like a fizz,
Particles seize the wind, Her substance His.
That I may master His darknesses,
I dip toward His disk; His eclipse my gain,
Spin the ball of plasma as, through His pane,
Consciousness compounded, met in my brain,
He surrounds Her Moon with His lion's mane.

DANIEL ORSINI

THE CHARIOT OF ARISTOTLE'S WHEELS

The circle divides; quaternal its rays—
The ground-plan of the Self—the *opus* plays
Like a floating isle or Theseus' maze.
When we enter His cave, the dark dismays.
We gather the world: the serpent that peels;
The spherical tomb of Hermes that heals;
In the vas all gold, the glass that anneals:
The chariot of Aristotle's wheels.

Self-heated, we incubate; glean like Ge
The substance of the stone: the weightless key.
Before we reach dry land, unless we flee,
Prone, we wash at the bottom of the sea.
I scan the Book of Life—from page to page,
The mythos where male and female engage;
Where sages pronounce and coheirs assuage
And still polarities like angels rage.

I have lived with You; eaten from Your plate
Cislunar manna; mingled like a mate;
Your cloudform ferried from another state,
I sift You that I may fulfill my fate
Even as a seed that basks in its shell—
Some embryo that feels its layers jell,
Such shards of light as Ge alone can swell
Enswathed in fluids, milk skin that we smell.

CHRIST ON EINSTEIN'S TRAM

A cyborg can spacewalk—unhinge his feet
Upon lunar soil, his astronaut's beat
Rippled as a stair: accordion's pleat,
Coheir's silicone sole, or endless sheet.
And thus Ge inveigles Her son at first;
With caustic beguiles him; then, with a burst,
Disfigures the victim: sacrosanct, curst,
The self-same *rebis* in Hermes submersed.

Gender is private, serpentine, obscure—
Some treasured obol through which we procure
His sapphirine power; spherical, pure,
Eden's contraband, which none may abjure:
Meme or mystagog; tesseract or cone;
Shriven substance: *Rubeus* in the clone
On His tablet etched, its animate stone—
Eternity's sigil—scrolled on His throne.

My soul gamonymous, my shaman warm;
My arms extended, my muscles aswarm;
My breasts curvaceous, an hourglass my form—
Serene as sunrise, yet rugged as storm,
Maria, who do *you* say that I am?
An atom like a gram; Euphrates' dram:
Heracleian magnet; His Paschal lamb:
Shepherd of Aries—Christ on Einstein's tram.

CIRCUMAMBIENT

I opened the hatch, stood up in my seat,
Then stepped outside, till, propelled by the heat,
I uncoiled my tether, dangled my feet,
Then floated there, exhilarated, fleet.
All life is real, Castor, when it is shown.
Lost in a body made of silicone,
My aim deliberate, I tossed my stone
To the other side. I banished my clone.

I near His altar; with a question to ask,
Leave at His door my alchemist's flask;
Genuflect, and then dedicate my mask.
With what have I been left? — *That* is the task.
I carry His image, the glyph of Earth:
A soul-spark; a scion; Shem's second birth:
His tabernacled Son; sublime His girth,
Sapphirine *rebis,* I savor His worth.

Present in the psyche, the Savior sleeps.
A stranger to dogma, His essence seeps
Even as an incense. — The symbol keeps
Till, from His temenos, the foetus leaps.
Urn like a vessel, capsule like a seed's,
The sapient Self, like His biped, breeds.
Ancient as the Sun or the Moon that feeds,
Circumambient, the *opus* proceeds.

CLAIM

Surprised by every molecule that hits,
The spiral galaxy that never quits,
And any nation that the weaver knits,
He incubates the egg, and there he sits,
As if, among the epochs that he tracked
In the seeding place that the Savior cracked,
From anthropoid to hierophant he stacked,
Then reconstructed an archaic fact.

Out of nothing he grew, nowhere his name
Except at midnight; in his dream a claim—
A glyph on a tablet: the Moon that came,
In Her stream His scion, photon or flame.
We journey in the vessel of the Sun;
Trail its clue; in the spheroid that He spun,
Ascertain His prey; Ouroboros stun,
Then mapquest the One on Möbius' run.

Who knows how it was, and who shall declare
That Creation is rare, and who shall care
That bodies dissemble that Spirits wear
Or metaverses tear in Saturn's lair?
In the Virgin's lap, made captive by love
He navigates Heaven; met by a dove,
Consoles the cyborg below and above,
In His capsule, warm as Robonaut's glove.

DANIEL ORSINI

CONTAINMENT AND THE COSMIC EDGE

Upraised in the cosmos that we explore—
Everything physical, and nothing more—
We process bosons, galaxies that pour,
Spears that vanish, and molecules that store.
Azure as the bead in a bowl of light
Demarcated by air, the hill is tight.
Still the world is edgeless—without a bight,
A continuum real in its own right.

Beyond the cuboid, I stretch out my hand.
As I pluck its string, I twine a new strand;
Nearer to Heaven than hues in the band,
Respond to its riddle; at my command,
Shaman in the lobe—uncanny atom—
Unwind in my mind Hephaestus' datum:
As if, spagyric, the bulk begat Him
Or else, like a point, some god had spat Him.

His Mother the Moon, His Father the Sun,
He tinctures His remnant. He is the One.
He enters His clay; that He may be done
And out of His body His Spirit spun,
He stirs in the vas such Monads as brim
Even as Adam, each spark and each limb,
The parts of the body behind the scrim,
All the souls of the world, contained in Him.

COSMIC DUST

From pre-solar grains or haloed gases,
Surface deposits on Earth's ice-masses,
Or *gegenschein* that nothing surpasses,
We sample such dust as Gaea classes.
Thus in the night sky, elliptical, green,
We can trace its path; through Ge's eyepiece glean—
With its band around the ecliptic seen—
Zodiacal light in capsules of sheen.

After the Big Bang, darkness without form,
Swollen, distended, clouds began to swarm,
Till matter coalesced, substance *that* warm
Its aspirations simmered in the storm
Like Gaea's tesseract, where spirals are,
Apertures to places that epochs bar:
Shells of infrared or Cheshires that char—
Globular clusters with smiles that yet jar.

Like colossal tides or moons that draw near
Or microfossils, ancient rocks their bier,
Both wave and particle, whole as I peer,
The cosmos is filled with objects not here.
And thus I suffuse my spin with a grin.
I stand on Ge's torus even as my twin.
An incandescent mist inside my skin,
I am still on the outside looking in.

COURTSHIP

In Gaea's house, where Unity once knocked,
We try each door that the Hubble unlocked:
Coal Sack and Cepheid, Cloverleaf clocked,
Like Centaurus A, by its dust ring blocked.
Ancient as a sage, a photon can fly
Across the aeons; the retina ply,
Encased in parsecs, Ge's numinous spy:
The spagyric foetus coiled in its eye.

We have trampled on the garment of shame;
Aberrant as matter, assign the blame;
Exalted at last by Hosea's claim,
Neither male nor female nor *rebis* name.
By beasts, and birds, and things that creep perplexed,
We script such a text as Ge has annexed—
Some sapphirine premise; no longer vexed,
The map of Her body, our muscles flexed.

When old stars in globular clusters merge,
Out of their ashes protoplanets surge
Even as particles that spheroids urge
Outside the horizon or, inside, purge.
Still galaxies slide or mix in the light,
As Hermes observes; to his smitten sight,
Courtship in the cosmos the strangest rite.
Like us he is not alone in the night.

THE CUSP OF SKILL

Pneumatic we rise; on the path of truth,
Each cyborg alone, each spouse in his booth
Ablaze with the fires of our stellar youth,
Begin at the Bang; with its serpent's tooth,
Resorb such flakes as migrate and then mill,
Like Oldowan scratch marks, tubers that fill,
Crystalline prisms, lanceolate spill,
Acheulian tools on the cusp of skill.

Fixated on the world, its model cast
Even as a bubble, sintered or glassed,
The artifex prays, while crucibles blast,
That the *lapis* stay—it has always passed.
He lifts from the vessel, amber its tint,
Kobolds; metal men; robonauts that squint,
Acrylic their helmets; star seeds that glint:
Creation's biped, *face set like a flint.*

Having sought to reach beyond humankind,
I ascertained the scroll that Ge had signed:
Hyphenate body, alchemystic mind,
Silicone *rebis.* By my SenSuit shrined,
Cislunar my nomad, thus I deployed
Hermes round and square, my astronaut buoyed
Even as an orphan—Thinsulate, cloyed,
Dazed in my moonship like a humanoid.

DANIEL ORSINI

DRILLING ON MARS

I journey into Space that I may find

A breathable atmosphere not less kind

Than even the skein that Clotho once twined.

I scan its scenario in my mind.

Extrapolar planets listed as stats,

I seek in isolated habitats

Ramjets; CubeSats; like disappearing cats,

Past Centauri, Ge's simulated plats.

While sail beaming, on my way to the light

Facing Gaea's plight, I enter the night.

Adjusted to the aether—Kepler's rite—

Pioneers, I master the art of flight.

And still I would cross to another strand.

Through some forgotten language: Mars' command

That Venus signs to my robotic hand,

In the ochre tract of Chryse I land.

In a patch of desert I test my will,

Hook up a screen that with data I fill,

Grab a lever at the back of the drill,

Signal to the U-Haul, and then I spill—

Amid a fine white dust—a starry hail

Like ice and rock, or gypsum in a pail,

Till, having weighed its scoop upon my scale,

I scrape its surface with my fingernail.

EPHESIAN SYMBOLS

A Kevlar scion, in his cap a plume,
Glass in his eye slot; qwiff that we exhume
Attired in silicone: android or groom,
Motion-captured, he wanders in the room.
Wound up and turned on, a machine that hops,
He whirs into action, and then he stops,
Like chiming quartz each parsec that he shops
Fed by a crystal even as he crops.

Beyond His font Ge's chthonic orphans lurk.
With awe on their faces, almost a quirk,
Like dactyls they steer yet never shirk.
Forged out of gold they help Him in His work.
Their eyes like wheels, without seeing they see.
Teachers of Orpheus, holders of the key,
They lend to His disciples, and to Ge,
Ephesian symbols, magic formulae.

Pneuma in the vessel; shadow in the lair:
Puer aeternus, riddle of the pair—
We search in Spacetime sigils that we share,
Some purer substance: weightless as the air,
Stone that incubates; binding as the sands,
Inwards of the head; intertwined its strands,
Sulphur, mercury, balsam in the bands,
The podium on which Our Savior stands.

EVANGELIST

We ask ourselves what the world is made of—
A quantum of light; Below and Above;
Particle colliders; Robonaut's glove—
We master its codes with infinite love.
We network Ge's android; our headgear donned,
Simulate its skein; its circuitry conned,
Describe its orbit; bi-ocular, bond;
Inhabit Spacetime in stations beyond.

As sealed as the knoll that its magus maps,
Ge's cyborg can, while its sensor adapts—
Since consciousness persists despite its gaps—
Apperceive Heaven even as it naps.
The priest that brackets both pleasure and pain
Tabernacles its subject, Gaea's swain—
Like soul from such blood as flows in the vein—
Some epiphenomenon of the brain.

In the sky nearby, a galaxy blooms:
Syzygies in lunar and solar rooms,
Ge's course gamonymous—both Bride's and Groom's.
How shyly the concept of selfhood looms.
Across the disk, in capsule or calèche,
We track a web as intricate as mesh;
At its omphalos, designate its crèche;
Raise its species as virtual as flesh.

EXTRACT OF THE MACROCOSM

I rise in the omniverse like a bead,

Lay the whole to His procreative seed.

A breed, then His scion, and then a creed,

Or perhaps a riff or only a reed,

I bridge all Spacetime to the Paschal Lamb;

Mighty as a mountain, small as a gram,

The *puer aeternus* crowned in His pram,

Become what I will and am what I am.

Formerly One, the hierophant presides;

A self-contained totality, divides

Between Heaven and Earth, and thus He bides:

Extract of the Macrocosm, He hides.

In the darkness of matter, sealed He came

Even as the *opus,* wholeness His aim

From below upwards; unfettered His claim:

Some primeval doctrine without a name.

In rock at first, in forebrow, or in mist,

The Self beyond the Ego, we subsist:

The offspring of the *rebis*—Hermes' tryst—

Or Ouroboros' circle with a twist.

An astronaut, the foetus in the lore,

He seems dimensional—flesh, and yet more:

Instinct; Tradition; Chiliasm's Four;

Embodiment as level as a door.

DANIEL ORSINI

FABRICATOR

We move without motion: The rock from bone
That rises in the fireball is not sown;
Like seas from Ymir's sweat, the sky His clone
Conceals His flesh: *the stone that is no stone.*
Knowledge is tacit: silence in the ear
Evokes the light the nearer that we peer.
Foam in the tunnel, silver in the spear,
Sulphur in the middle, salt in the tear.

In the interim he struggles to speak.
He achieves coherence and is not meek.
Bubble in the chaos, magnet in the beak,
Spark in the semen, breath-soul in the Sikh—
He indwells each subject that he discerns:
Tipler's subset, radiation that burns,
Shem's enigma: the manikin that learns.
Between bulk and air, the world-wheel yet turns.

Melting into Him the Mind yet commits
To the selfsame Spouse that the Bridegroom knits.
Reborn in the Sun, in the Moon he sits.
Extended the believer never quits.
As moist as the body that He has planned
Or, palpable, such skein as He has scanned—
Both hidden and manifest—*He has spanned*
The unity of the whole with His hand.

FIXATED ON MARS

It spins like a marble, leans on its run
Like Heaven's astronaut or, having spun,
Like the disk in the eye; till it is One,
It arcs through its orbit around the sun.
Still I tilt elsewhen; on Möbius' strip,
Moonlike, cratered, it stirs me as I trip.
A storyteller, its name on my lip,
Fixated on Mars I enter the ship.

We join at its threshold, like avatars,
A fleet of spacecraft and robotic cars,
Then peer like specters or evening stars
On boulder-sized rocks that dominate Mars.
We prospect from orbit, without a gate,
Sulfates in the chasma, craters that mate,
Lobate débris aprons; next on our slate,
Giant canyons layered early or late.

We search its site: our kinship with the light;
Lift, as we navigate both day and night
In shroud or bunting, our own planet's wight,
Till, clear-sighted, we ascertain the rite.
We wane and wax with the Martian seasons;
Scoop its soil—like Ge's daughters *and* Ge's sons,
Gravity and ice His coheir's reasons,
Or wayfarer's dream, or only treason's.

GATEKEEPER

I approach a door archival as fate,
Insert the phantom key, unlatch the gate,
Enter the temple like vessels that mate:
Jachin and Boaz. — My own candidate
Projected into space, I pace the Sun.
Entwined in its skein, I yet trace its run,
Then search its source-point: nascent in the dun
Behind the stars, the stillness of the One.

In the dreamtime of His symbol I pause,
Then like a silhouette shrouded in gauze—
The foetus in its case without a clause
To sanction its laws—solicit His cause.
The uncanny Sun rests, and still I spy.
A tilted planet circles in the sky
Till darkness descends, impartial or shy,
Even as the lid of a closing eye.

As if I scaled Her like some biped twirled,
Then at the threshold of the mare hurled
Weightless as the membrane in which I curled—
This is the chaos that we call the world,
Both entrance and exit as near as snow
That swam upon the waters, Sol aglow
In the midst of Night, the womb that we know
In at which to come, out of which to go.

GATEWAY

We search such a world as the Sun devised:
An acidic soup, its spores fossilized,
Then found in space rocks; micro-fungi prized;
Or even Planet Nine, hypothesized;
Spaceship or Monad: foetus in its purse;
Panspermia comet-borne—texts *that* terse,
Like nuanced lacunae, hosts that rehearse
Scatter like sparks throughout the universe.

To planets that orbit the globe we cling:
The Galilean satellites—a string
Like pebbles or dust or moons in a ring.
They thread through my cosmic eye and then spring.
Spacewalker or wire-, below you the mire,
In boot or shoe, when you enter the gyre,
Set to go higher, before you the pyre,
Astronaut or sire, you do go higher.

Obsessed by a prophet to mysteries prone,
In Him the doors of the solstices sown,
I cross a threshold that His coheirs own.
From cave to cone I pass to the unknown,
Scour the sky, and then sapphirine attain,
Ensconced in His capsule or in His wain,
Circuits that range from a house to a skein
Colossal almost as the human brain.

THE HEAVENLY JOURNEY OF THE SHAMAN

I orbit the moon till day and night pall;

Float into my pouch; then, strapped to the wall

Even as a bean, a plant, or a ball,

Spagyric once more, occupy my caul.

And then I awake; till the world-egg crack,

My body begins to grow from the back.

Curved like a tail, or coat upon its rack,

I lift my hand to my mouth and then track.

Because he brings *the coming of the Light,*

He enters Creation; despite its blight,

Venusian as the Moon, his spacesuit white,

He dominates the cosmos in the night.

Having climbed from his craft, unseen his face,

He scans the rock; a foot restraint his base,

He tugs at the boulder; samples its trace;

Manipulates an asteroid in space.

Elusive as Spirit or Motion's air,

Cross-beams' quaternity or else a pair,

Sabaean a temple inside a square,

A sevenfold star he circles its stair.

He spins in the heavens; without a knot,

Undertakes the journey; capsules his tot,

In his mind the *rebis,* cyborg or bot,

Like Ouroboros, compressed to a dot.

HERE BE DRAGONS

Nomads in the mare we seek the Son,
The Spirit in the moon, and then the One;
In the interim, Ouroboros spun,
Corpus mysticum on Möbius' run.
Our vessel spherical, foursquare our fate,
We brood in the capsule; rebirth the bait—
His brazen serpent, source-point of our state—
Hither and thither, upraised we rotate.

When Adam scattered skein, he scoured his brain;
Abraham charted Moriah's terrain,
Elias His wheel, Maria Her swain,
Till through Her navel Yahweh ran His fane.
Amber His hair, His staff like a petal
Floating free out of furnace or kettle,
The Son of Man—Hephaestan His fettle—
He pours from His fire like molten metal.

The dragon of Babel lies down in his bed.
Having fed on manna, wingless yet wed,
By angels ministered, Christ in the bread,
He swallows his body into his head.
Ge's essence animate, substance he bleeds—
Like a rope of words—a stone's or a bead's
Moist *albedo,* Light's metabolized screeds,
Ashen extracts—*everything that he needs.*

A HOST-STAR IN DRACO

A rocky giant, a version of Earth,
Its host-star in Draco; defying its worth,
Worlds lit by auroras; as at a birth,
The surge of planets: We measure their girth.
We spot each phantom with a telescope—
Like Moon and Earth, some tied, as with a rope,
In the Goldilocks Zone, where probes yet grope
Among the red dwarfs even as we cope.

We ride a rocket into space, then slice
Skein encased in a shell of water ice,
Jupiter's Europa—spin of the dice:
Neptune's own Triton. Moonshots still entice.
Soon we pace the speed of the solar wind—
Layers of matter: the chromosphere, pinned,
Exotic as our craft or tamarind
Or the berry that Ge cannot rescind.

Though pixel by pixel and row by row,
Time's pictures extend us, and thus we show,
When the Sun engulfs us, where shall we go?
At eclipse the sun in the moon may stow.
From oxygen and carbon we are made . . .
Sodium, iron, zinc, as Spacetime bade.
His body intact, transcendent as jade,
From dust the foetus forms, an even trade.

THE JESUS OF PSYCHOANALYSIS

Born in a stable, entwined like a wave,
Baptized at the Jordan, where He would lave
His apostles like scions, stave by stave
Jesus bucketed souls beyond the grave.
When Heaven opened, the Savior went up
Out of the water; transfigured, would sup
In Gaea's Cenacle; then, with a Cup,
Conquered Time and Mephistopheles' pup.

As if at His shrine, in many vases
His afterbirth yet preserved, He braces.
Having met His match, His body races.
Detached from Himself and all His traces,
Jesus basks in her ointment. — As she nears,
She drinks Him in; with her eyes and her ears,
Eroticizes Him; till, through Her tears,
Toward the foetal life of His tomb He steers.

If we could but find, as we endeavor,
One solid point, a long enough lever—
Some rule of thumb, heuristic, whatever—
We might from ourselves His semblance sever.
Fixated on Him, his witness a bird,
He climbs the sycamore; his sign secured,
Commutes his flesh; transfers it to the Word—
The breath of Jesus: what Zacchaeus heard.

DANIEL ORSINI

LIGHT OF THE EYE

The world is but a sign; that we may live,
Presents itself to us; through vas or sieve,
Evokes the Absolute, and thus we give—
We re-present its dream; demonstrative,
Map its terrain at the back of the brain:
Transparent windows, archetypes that reign
Above and below—moonchild in the wain,
Both Self and shaman: kobold in the vein.

The sage, assembled, dries over a stone
His heated heartbeat; hyaline, alone,
Prepares the altar; consecrates its clone;
Extracts the cislunar soul from its bone.
He concocts *a pup of celestial hue,*
Temples and obelisks, disks that accrue,
Secret sulphur that hierophants construe,
In the one thing hidden, all metals true.

I saw a rocket like Mercury fly;
Atom by atom, Ge's semblances vie:
Silver in Cabeus, plume in the sky,
In the cloud a foetus: light of the eye.
Spacetime fostered, Singularity pearled,
The cortex bulges; its frontal lobe furled,
The way that *we* fold it, upright or curled,
Is the only way that we know the world.

LOCAL BUBBLE

For ten million years or for a a day,
We have traveled in a cloud, and here we stay:
Egg-shaped, elliptical, a ghostly gray—
The Orion Arm of the Milky Way.
Like Geminga's remnant or Clotho's thrum,
The four-finger span and, chthonic, the thumb,
Matter light years across—spagyric gum—
In the Local Bubble we go or come.

Ashes from the Big Bang having dispersed,
We speculate why supernovae burst.
What shall we say then—that Chaos is first?
We enter the retort; Hermes submersed,
He floats in the flask, his *rebis* elate
In a bright dress of blossom: Heaven's mate—
Ge's coheir—implicate; wholeness its slate,
The omniverse itself predestinate.

In traditions of his ancestors wrapped,
Truths into which solar archetypes tapped—
As if with *his* life all life had been capped—
He grasped the tiny sleeve of skin and flapped
With his instrument; where its blade had spun,
Gathered Sight's gamonymus into One
In some supracelestial place; that done,
Entwined the cosmos, both moonchild and sun.

DANIEL ORSINI

THE MAN IN THE MOON

Born at the crescent, at the waning lost,
He points to the Messiah; haloed, crossed,
Reborn as the Bridegroom, His body tossed,
He infills the spheroid, Earthshine the cost.
As He scales the cavern, drives His calèche,
Then spans such clusters as nomads enmesh,
Baptized in water, debtor to the flesh,
He empties Her: *kenosis* at the crèche.

He opens the hatch; stands up in his seat;
Then, stepping aside, propelled on his beat
Beyond Gaea's capsule, hand-held his heat,
His spacesuit bulky, walks without a cleat.
His soul like an eye—the loop that you splice—
His Phoebe summons him; doubled His dice,
Satellites magnetize; breccias entice;
In the vas of the moon all men die twice.

As if I had found some numinous tract
In tunnels of the moon that Gaea stacked,
The *rebis* scrolled, and the hierophant cracked:
Astral symbolon, autonomous fact,
He touches down lightly; expands Her threads
In the Cayley Plains, till the man that weds
Upon such soil as Her basin embeds,
Sets down his boot—Sight's imprint—in the treads.

MASTERMIND

A world evolves that purifies the heart.
Like the breath of the Spirit, clouds that start,
Or the great south wind that mystagogues chart,
Its source is the retort, a hidden art.
Its wheels quaternal, like faces that furl,
A dragon arises; in a sea of pearl,
An *imago mundi;* God in the swirl,
Once perfected, it becomes like a whirl.

He clothes Him like *the stone that is no stone,*
Such gamonymous matter as we own,
Like His far-flung omphalos, zone by zone,
In harmony with Ge or else alone.
Ethereal clone, diversified groom,
He combines all colors: subtile His tomb—
Matrix or uterus, skein like a room—
The spagyric foetus spun in His womb.

We fan in the brain the fire that began
In the fettered cosmos; despite its ban,
Sol's entelechy; immanent His plan,
The New Jerusalem in the inner man.
We link the torus; tabulate the spin;
Adrift in the residue of the din,
Our souls projected, aspirants of tin
Rotund as Adam Secundus, begin.

DANIEL ORSINI

A METHANE SNOW

My fingers fully formed, stern in my sac,
With ears and eyelids I begin to stack:
Embryo first, then foetus at the crack,
My skeleton alive, no longer slack,
I spiral in her womb, and then I stall;
Balloon into my birth, and then I fall;
Talisman, omen, diadem in the ball,
In Jesus' nightgown push, and then I call.

Amid such twine as ravels in the street,
I track a cloud, His soul-spark, and then, fleet,
Like Heaven's dactyl wafted in his seat
From Clotho's skein, the scion in the pleat.
He offends the flesh, then wakens the soul:
The Pole in the sky, the Tree on the knoll,
Like Abraham's cube or coin in the roll:
Puer aeternus, He evokes the whole.

Sown gamonymus: sod that Time bedecks
With a silver streak that his coil connects,
In his spacesuit dressed, the astronaut treks
The same metallic dust that he collects.
Despite galactic cosmic rays we go—
We travel through an interstellar glow
In the D-brane: volcanoes that we know,
Salmon-tinted Pluto, a methane snow.

THE MOON IN TRANSITION RAISED TO THE SUN

We pre-breathe in the airlock; spacewalk; stand;
Straddle the chaos on Möbius' strand;
With inch-worming arm and two-fingered hand,
Each task yet choreographed, scripted, planned,
Unhook attached components; hoist; alight
That we may hitch a ride, without a bight,
Upon a foot restraint. — By day or night,
Earth orbit serves as our construction site.

He houses four cameras in his head;
For depth perception one more, infrared,
Mounted in his mouth as if Saturn fed
On Gaea's biped even as a thread.
He controls his joints; like other ringers
With tendon-driven, robotic fingers,
Erects the station; repairs cracked stringers;
Seized by sunrise, at its threshold lingers.

If through the bubble the astronaut peers
And in the vessel like a foetus steers
And rises and ascends throughout the years
And reaches the *rebis* in flames and tears,
Then water *is* fire; in the cauldron spun—
After the *albedo* (the yellow shun):
The sole white color that leads to the One—
The moon in transition raised to the sun.

THE PATH OF LEAST ACTION

Brethren, we see with the eyes of the heart:
Vestiges, images, hierophant's art,
Primordial atoms that ravel smart,
Cluster galaxies that satellites chart.
And still the cosmos hangs upon its hook.
In the icy light we squint and then look.
Spacetime's Leviathan, beak of a rook,
Like an alchemist in the heat we cook.

Both black and saffron, mottled red and brown,
Metallic inmate, neither verb nor noun,
Does it matter to you that we shall drown?
Heavy is the body that bears the crown.
By morning, at the furnace, bolt upright,
Amid the stench of graves I reached the light;
Entwined the funnelweb; wound toward its height,
Sped the azure Savior, primrose then white.

As if I had said to the god Who goes,
Or selfsame multiverse the god Who grows,
Sum of infinity the god Who flows,
How may I realize the god Who knows?
A foetus in the googolsphere I slept,
A wanderer through hyperspace I crept,
An astronaut that large adept I stepped,
Into the path of least action I leapt.

PSALTER

He stands on the round chaos; holds the scales;
Sown from antinomies, fecund he fails
Even as the Moon or Sun that She trails
Before She transmutes and then She bails.
Nothing prospers; until hatched from His brain,
Nothing is begotten: in a land of pain,
Without end or aim, scattered His skein—
Both content and context—the King lies slain.

We slumber in matter and thus we turn
Upon a rocket until, past its burn,
Faster than Light we ride and, while we yearn,
Conjure the wingèd soul out of its urn.
We shoulder our way, the air like a hiss,
Or tuning fork, or Ouroboros' kiss,
Or Ge's conundrum: either *quid* or *quis*—
A quality, not a hypostasis.

I divide the world even as I run
Into Heaven's four quarters: whole or none,
The sole quaternity that Clotho spun.
I pause. Since all things proceed from the One,
I near the temenos with my psalter.
Like the Sun-god or Heracles' vaulter,
I scan as I span—I do not falter—
The line from the front door to the altar.

DANIEL ORSINI

REBIS

Like a bubble that shimmers in its pan,
Or seahorse that floats amid frond or fan,
Or ball of cells that from its roots began,
He sought to be neither woman nor man,
But both these sexes: hybrid of the same;
A fructified seed; either fire or flame—
Quaternity's startlement: frame by frame,
Scion or *Rebis,* First Adam by name.

As the soil that, sprung from its furrow, grunts,
So, Typhon pursuing him, Pisces shunts
In the wettest place that the foetus fronts.
We become a child and a fish at once.
We enter the omniverse; monads strewn,
We navigate the belly of the moon;
Traverse its mare; twine at perilune
In Clotho's net, and then cruise its cocoon.

Liquid metal its guise, His cyborg spun
From heavenly skein, crowned Mother and Son,
He casts us in a mold till we are One.
The distance between them pain that we shun,
She steals from Her dais stones that we swap:
Thumb in the heart or holon that we crop
As moist as salt; rotundum that we prop
Between His spouses, at mid-point we stop.

RITE

Even as the photon, phantom its size;
Velocity without place: quantum eyes,
We indwell the cosmos, surveil its rise,
Fabricate its foam, advocate its lies.
From an ancient gas cloud the first star rears,
Cluster swallows cluster, the Dragon steers,
Abstraction surfaces, Hyperspace sears,
And then, like Ouroboros, disappears.

Space is not vacant; wind-generated,
A bubble persists that Time created.
Gaea mated, the heliosphere sated,
The interstellar hierophant fated,
A rocket rises: Venus in the dunes
Transits into twilight till Saturn's boons—
Like alphabet rings and habitable moons—
With Jupiter reckon in Castor's runes.

He places his right arm into the sleeve
And then his left arm and then by His leave
Consecrates the Host, and then with a weave
Eastward he steps, and His breath-souls conceive.
I scan a wheel of stars, construe the white,
Pursue the galaxies night after night.
Because I was raised in the Roman rite,
At my threshold I still invite the kite.

THE ROUND DANCE OF THE STARS

Impulsive as the sun His body slants.
Even as particles pending advance,
He peers down His eye slot, and thus He pants.
To each and all it is given to dance.
We clasp His hand, and then we form a ring.
Begotten we beget, and still we sing.
Ecstatic we never usurp His string.
To Paradox and Mystery we cling.

Without a uniform meaning I sift,
Both Self and sacrificer. — Heaven's gift
The Messiah's Mass, the Eucharist's rift:
I will be wounded, His mirror, I shift.
I approach His room; its point my center,
Ingest; assimilate; cosmic, enter
Like His disciples or priests that mentor
Or Prophetissa or stars that spent her.

Like the Seraphim, my foam the driest,
Or sidewise Adam, my fate the wryest,
Or saffron Savior, no longer biased,
I scour the skein from lowest to highest.
Quicksilver scion, captive of the white,
I roam Her mare; insolent as sight,
Photons yet twine me. — Like heron and kite,
Minerals fluoresce in the presence of light.

SCHRÖDINGER'S CAT

A cat in a box may live or not live.
Ge tangles its life: a wave through a sieve.
She ascertains each photon that we give,
The smile of Ge's Cheshire distributive.
Superposition the state that we flee
Even in Limbo, by Heaven's decree,
We yet twine the globe, like Her shaman see,
Collapse its skein into slope rock or scree.

It was not a house, a cloud, or a jar—
A drop of liquid absorbed by a spar:
Residual coupling. — Space like a scar,
He set his course by the path of a star.
Polaris the point, around it he turned.
His heart Hermetic, in its vas he churned;
Absorbed such archetypes as he discerned,
Then reached the *rubedo,* dawn that he burned.

A borderline concept the Self is wry
Even as the world; its cornerstone shy—
Totality in parts—the proven eye
Fixates on the symbol until we die.
He forms through illusion; matter purloined,
Substance hypostatized, Ge's *rebis* coined,
He enters Her navel; Adam thus groined,
Swallows the nature to which he is joined.

DANIEL ORSINI

SCINTILLA'S SCAN

Complicit, we crown an archaic king;

Scourge even as we mock Him, then with a sling

Suspend the body, elevate Him, sing,

Cut open His heart till its serum spring.

As particles gather, Substance the key,

He transforms Himself; exemplar of glee,

With but a codicil and then a plea,

He leads His nomad to His solar tree.

As subtile as a god, His trace unnerves.

Hermes yet exists; quaternal He curves.

He does not trespass on other preserves.

The Self, incorruptible, never swerves.

Its point Archimedean, Heaven's jot

Surpasses the ego, upends its tot,

Unravels Ouroboros like a knot.

What now I am seen to be I am not.

Archetypes abound: the Bread in His palm,

A ray of sunlight, and Gilead's balm.

I will be united His avid psalm,

Eternity's hybris His only qualm,

The Savior hosts His Bride, pursues His plan,

Upraises like each gamonymous man

Cedar, pine, and cypress, then scours His clan

With His consummate eye: scintilla's scan.

SCION

An astronaut wanders where he may list.
To savor the quest, he searches its gist:
His unit tethered—tyranny or tryst—
Hephaestus engenders him in His fist.
Like a shard through fingers sprung from its zone,
Windmill or wheel; projectile like a stone;
Even Ge's shapeshifter, hidden or shown,
Gravity's planet, Earth upheaves its own.

And thus I ascend; spasmodic my flight,
I push against my straps from left to right.
My awareness heightened like second sight,
Saturn's first-stage engines, clustered, ignite.
The image of Castor, staid in the herm,
Recedes in my eye till resolute, firm,
Skein's Ouroboros I curl like a worm,
Spacewalk, then carry my foetus to term.

Cosmos in the cauldron, island in space,
Designer universe without a face,
Ge's gamonymous law its only base,
Sun no less than moon, he describes the race:
Random as a bullet from a pistol,
Or, rolled in parchment, proximal, distal,
Layered its art, a pasteboard from Bristol,
Scion regimented as a crystal.

SCOUT

He searches the Moon, where history lies—
A portal to its crust; between his eyes,
White light of the Tao; the 'square inch' its size,
Envisions Ge's outpost beyond the skies:
Some multi-ringed crater; basin or bluff
Bombarded by débris; ejecta's slough
Like seas of basalts. — Fundamental, rough,
Hermes' lunar visits are not enough.

I glimpse a shape like a Catherine-wheel.
Assailed by dust and by one star *that* real,
I fasten to its ray, and then I deal.
I display my shuttlesuit like a seal.
Salt- or sun-point, I frame my origin:
Center *and* circumference; bean in the bin;
Hephaestus' scion—Asclepius' jinn,
Like Phoebe's twin, transconscious in the tin.

I switch on a bulb in a darkened room,
The delay so slight before light can loom
On an opposite wall, in space or womb
I contemplate Ge's Andromedan gloom.
As if the God had sped me in a pram
Like Castor or Pollux, foetus or gram,
Or—prefigured at the sign of the Ram—
Rebis or Lamb, I can guess where I am.

THE SMOKE-HOLE OF THE TENT

We platform the station, gateway to Mars;
Construct a habitat in space that chars;
In cislunar orbit, like avatars,
Exalt the spheroid and then search the stars.
We board NASA's capsule; like Hermes curl;
Capture an asteroid; redirect; hurl;
Amid lava bleeds and craters that furl,
Spagyric foetus, in the chaos whirl.

He rides to infinity; seeks its dot;
In void or omphalos—First Adam's plot—
Pursues His origin; unties its knot;
Locates His slot: iota, yod, or jot.
From Her bobbin, the Spinner that He lent,
She winds Her thread, the weave with which She blent
The crown of the head, the Sun that He sent,
Eye of the dome, and *smoke-hole of the tent.*

I draw each day a picture in my mind,
Like Adam Kadmon, before and behind
A concrete icon that His coheirs signed,
Psychologists exhumed, and saints enshrined.
Creation sequenced above and below—
A sower, His seed, and rivers that flow—
The Shulamite dips, in Her damp a glow:
Wash me, and I shall be whiter than snow.

DANIEL ORSINI

SPACETIME'S WIGHT

They wash Him then rinse, sprinkle then immerse,
Untie His attachments and then asperse
The remnants of His body; steer the hearse
Toward His wall of jasper or else His curse:
Some liminal pathway, a starker rite
Than the node at new moon that strains His sight
Before Maria holds Him and Her Light
Consolidates in darkness Spacetime's wight.

His fiber strewn, a microscopic thread,
Elaborate textile, He is not dead.
He weaves into tendons, muscles that wed,
Membranes that multiply, and fingers that spread.
The length of the forehead, He dwells in the face,
The field of the square inch. Precinct or trace,
The Spinner yet burns; the Moon in His case,
Pursues His race at Ouroboros' pace.

We edit His skein like a rumored pain,
A symptom in the chest till we complain,
A lesion on the skin, a scar, a stain—
The *semblance* of the Savior: Gaea's swain.
When chaos advances, pictures convince:
A lance that glints, a unicorn that sprints,
A circle, a spiral, a shroud that hints,
On the retina a patchwork of tints.

THE SPEAR OF ARCHYTAS

Like Castor and Pollux, astronauts twined,
We share a habitat both sealed and signed.
And still we follow where humanoids wind—
Some rarefied globe, its contents enshrined.
As if in a picture, its canvas stained;
Like Ge's orb-weaver's web, its skin yet veined
By colossal spirals; the cosmos gained,
The magus fabricates and is contained.

Sometimes a missile darts across the skies—
Spear of Archytas; stone that, heated, dries;
On shuttle stacks loaded, boosters that rise.
Edgeless, limitless, infinite in size,
Space is but a body: crystals or spheres
Like atoms in the void, or fire that sears,
Or Gog's gamonymus: serpent that rears,
Or Mind that toward itself, aetheric, steers.

Tolerant of choice, yet to discord prone,
We cultivate the faith that we have known
Even as a code; experience sown,
Rehearse the one zone that hierophants own.
As photons proliferate, beam by beam
Hermes hard-wired, embedded in the scheme,
We collapse the wave; the Son in the stream,
Anoint the *rebis;* apprehend the dream.

SPLITTING THE EARTH WITH A STRAIGHT FOOT

Circumambient, like His cosmic eye,
Or crystals flung from the vault of the sky,
Or *puer aeternus,* capsuled I fly,
Without rust I waken, and still I ply.
Bound by a thread, across the world I wend;
Spun from Clotho's spool, even as I spend,
I see ahead the unspeakable pend
And then the beginning begin to end.

Sown from the ash, the mother of lances,
He squints at the stars, motionless dances,
Beats the air that the plover enhances,
Walks upon the moon and thus advances.
Elsewhen, through its lacerating demise,
The quilted universe shall yet arise;
Impalpable its point, to His surprise,
The biped, though He dies, increase His size.

A girdle of shells; the belt of the stars;
Intermezzo of winds; with heat that chars,
The breath of the Spirit; sunships with tars
Translocated, the experience jars.
Like the trumpeter in search of a sound,
Or, born into His star, the shaman crowned,
With a straight foot the foetus splits the ground,
Then enters the womb of the Earth renowned.

STORYBOARD

Wearing magic glasses, the shaman twines

A triad of atoms, and then he binds.

When Oxygen falters, Hydrogen finds

The globe that beaming in the eyeslot winds.

The world that we weave is as strange as waves,

Its binary choices even as staves

Or, incorporeal, those Forms in caves

Or, in the slit, the paradox that saves.

Like pixels on a screen, patterns recur,

Appear, disappear, evolve, and then stir.

A convoy like clusters that sliding slur

Or syllables that breathe or else never were,

The cosmos stretches: recursive as sheets,

Unfolds into Gaea; compiled, secretes;

Implicates the spheroid; displays its pleats;

Scatters Clotho's thrum, and the loop repeats.

I had not known what the world would become—

A broth; then a template; like gum with gum,

Maria's Spagyric, Unity's sum

As large as a star, as small as a thumb.

Within the four quarters I sought to roam

Infinity's circle; a strip of foam;

A temenos simple enough to comb.

Yet I never did find my way back home.

TRAPEZE

Created from the dust, Adam was first
Till *Adam secundus*. The God-man nursed;
Then, at the river, His scion submersed,
From Zion's cenacle the biped burst.
Conscious as the ego, cosmic the Self
Multiplies like Being; from point to elf,
Mystery fascinates, History's pelf—
The foetus in the room—Maria's twelfth.

Master of Desire, He buckets the souls;
Pours into a mill in the form of scrolls
Upon cloven tongues the Word that He doles.
And still at Emmaus the Savior strolls.
Twin of two natures, transparent He seems
The Guest that banquets, the Body that beams,
The Sacrifice that His hierophant dreams
Even as Christ the Redeemer redeems.

I balance my body; reach toward the wire;
Gravity's point the gist of my desire,
I lower my hips; bend my knees; suspire;
Spacetime's intimate, re-enter the mire.
My phantom positioned, I sway then swerve.
Imbedded in aether, my feet yet curve,
Execute, stabilize, with suede preserve
More than the walker: the braid that I serve.

THE WATER THAT DOES NOT MAKE THE HANDS WET

It drips from the sun and produces gold.
Like the heat in the moon, the senses hold—
Among the archetypes that Ge foretold—
The radical moisture that Venus doled:
A solar sulphur. — Caught in Typhon's net,
Living stones exude a heavenly sweat:
Like the redness of the Egyptian Set,
The water that does not make the hands wet.

I name such glyphs as prefigure the Light:
Caelum, Elixir, Mother of the Night,
Balsam, Homunculus, Hermaphrodite.
Then, nomad, I add my stone to the site.
From below upwards His circle my goal
And then His temple, Ouroboros whole,
I overlap, interpenetrate, scroll,
Till I give my body back to its soul.

Outside Her womb like a thumbling I grope.
The sky above me I ravel my rope,
Lasso its mirror, implicate its trope,
Eyeball Creation, then compass its cope.
A scion having eyes yet seeing not,
I interweave Her skein like clouds that clot
Or rubeous tincture or yod or jot
Or navel's fold or Eternity's knot.

WAXING IN LUNA INTO THE NATURE OF THE SUN

He saw a crater and then a boulder;
Both ridge and rim; then, over his shoulder,
A shape like a peak; its valley older,
Without a shadow its surface colder.
He did not hover or drop to the ground;
Maneuvering, traversed over the mound;
At the edge of the basin wended, wound,
Then landed his module without a sound.

He raked lunar rock chips; recoiled perplexed;
Assailed his own shadow; his muscles flexed,
Hauled his seismometer; a gnomon; next,
A rack for his tools, then raveled the text.
And then he returned, his scion revised,
As if, dipped in waters and thus baptized,
He reached from Above to Below surprised,
His rite experienced, not strategized.

We cincture His tunic, then climb His Cross;
Like *foetus spagyricus* crowned in dross,
Advocate His sulphur; recount His loss;
Give to Cerberus such coins as we toss.
Even as opposites rise in the stave,
We watch through each eye His particle wave.
Devotion, knowledge, and Love alone save.
Woman and dragon embrace in the grave.

THE WOMAN IN THE MOON

Like the night, subliminal as a dream;
In mirrors of the heart, as mothers deem,
Glitter still compulsive, archetypes teem.
We fasten His semblance without a seam.
In baptismal waters that coheirs bless,
Or pail or *opus,* afloat we caress—
Since all Creation wears Her feather-dress—
Selene, Mary, with Horus-eyes Bes.

Nomadic the Moon, the abode of souls,
Buckets the hierophant; above Her knolls,
Circles the omphalos, signals, cajoles,
Pours from Her vessel even as She scrolls.
She balances His fate; incrusts His belts;
Enswathed like a priestess in dripping pelts,
Prepares His mantle; at sight of Him melts;
Transpierces Her bridegroom, then binds His welts.

Like an artist, outside and inside blent,
She fashioned a cradle and then a tent.
Sleep surrounded them wherever they went,
Aeons of memory, and then a scent.
She found within Herself an inner Sun.
Among the pine trees whispering She spun;
Then, Heaven's skein transplanted, having won,
Subject and object twined, said *It is done*.

NOTES AND COMMENTS

THE ROUND DANCE OF THE STARS:
NOTES AND COMMENTS
Daniel Orsini

Amber His hair: the gleaming yellow *hair* of the post-incarnate Christ, the Son of Man enthroned in His Heavenly ministry as Great High Priest. Cf. Rev. 1.14—"'The hair of his head was white as snow-white wool [. . .]"—in *The New English Bible with the Apocrypha* (1961; New York: Oxford UP, 1972). Subsequent Biblical citations are from this ecumenical text. *Here Be Dragons*

And still at Emmaus the Savior strolls: Having risen from the dead, Jesus walked with two disciples "to a village called Emmaus, which lay about seven miles from Jerusalem,'" and "'explained the scriptures'" to them. See Luke 24.13-14, 32. As "an embodiment of the God-image" (39) and as a symbol of both "the mystic Adam" (36) and "the transcendental self" (62), Christ, "being clothed in figures," is—according to St. Ephrem the Syrian (c. AD 306-373)—"the bearer of types" (140). C. G. Jung broaches these ideas, along with "the changing of the natures" (166), in *Aion: Researches into the Phenomenology of the Self,* trans. R. F. C. Hull (1959; Princeton: Princeton UP, 1969). *Trapeze*

Because he brings *the coming of the light:* In medieval alchemy, Mercurius is both "the Logos become world" and an analogue of Christ. Thus, "Since Mercurius is often called *filius,* his sonship is beyond question. He is therefore like a brother to Christ and a second son of God, though in point of time he must be accounted the elder and the first-born." In effect, "He heralds, as [Venus] the morning star does, only much more directly, the coming of the light" (C. G. Jung, *Alchemical Studies,* trans. R. F. C. Hull [1967; Princeton: Princeton UP, 1983] 222-23). Still, in this poem, the "Heavenly Shaman" is not just Mercurius; rather, he is also the second Adam (i.e., the Pauline Christ) and His present-day counterpart, the spiritually indwelt NASA astronaut—the "Tao [that] grows out of the individual" (53). *The Heavenly Journey of the Shaman*

the belt of the stars: i.e., the three *stars* of Orion's *belt*—Mintaka, Alnilam, and Alnitak—in the night sky, a familiar asterism associated in ancient Greece with the mythical hunter Orion and in ancient Egypt with Osiris, "who died periodically and was revived by the flooding of the Nile" (Sune Engelbrektson, *Stars, Planets, and Galaxies* [New York: Ridge-Bantam, 1975] 46). *Containment and the Cosmic Edge*

the berry that Ge cannot rescind: i.e., the grape—hence, in this poem, the irrevocable Eucharistic wine. *A Host-Star in Draco*

between his eyes / White light of the Tao [TOW]; the 'square inch' its size: In *Alchemical Studies,* "the central white light" of *the Tao* "dwells in the 'square inch' or in the 'face,' that is, between the eyes" (25). In other words, the universal Christ locates His kingship in the mind of each coheir: "a higher spiritual being [. . .] is invisibly born in the individual, a pneumatic body which is to serve as a future dwelling [. . .]" (51-52). See also Gal. 2.20: "I have been crucified with Christ: the life I now live is not my life, but the life which Christ lives in me [. . .]," along with the note on *The field of the square inch* given below. *Scout*

the Body that beams: See John 8.12: "Once again Jesus addressed the people: 'I am the light of the world. No follower of mine shall wander in the dark; he shall have the light of life.'" *Trapeze*

***A borderline concept* the Self is wry / Even as the world:** In *Psychology and Alchemy,* trans. R. F. C. Hull (1953; Princeton: Princeton UP, 1993), C. G. Jung reminds us that, "Owing to the fundamentally indefinable nature of human personality, the self must remain a borderline concept, expressing a reality to which no limits can be set" (355n13). *Schrödinger's Cat*

Born at the crescent, at the waning lost: a synopsis of the birth and death of Mary's Son—in this stanza, the lifespan of Jesus, the waxing and waning moonchild. *The Man in the Moon*

Born in a stable, entwined like a wave: The speaker refers to the quantum Christ described by a specific wavefunction—i.e., here, by the units of information encoded in an isolated system of particles and "collapsed" by the observer into reality. The alternate reading is *enshrined like a wave. The Jesus of Psychoanalysis*

bosons (BOH-sahnz): subatomic particles, each boson a "hypothetical packet of energy [that] has two units of spin." The term suggests "hidden symmetries of unseen dimensions," an idea that Michio Kaku underscores in *Hyperspace: A Scientific Odyssey through Parallel Universes, Time Warps, and the Tenth Dimension* (New York: Oxford UP, 1994) 144. *Containment and the Cosmic Edge*

bot: here, the shortened form of the word *robot. The Heavenly Journey of the Shaman*

Both round and square: C. G. Jung explains that, even in the Middle Ages, the soul, like the Moon, was "believed to be round" (*Mysterium Coniunctionis: An Inquiry into the Separation and Synthesis of Psychic Opposites in Alchemy,* trans. R. F. C. Hull [1963: Princeton: Princeton UP, 1989] 140). Here, of course, the speaker refers, with equal emphasis, to "the four quarters of the world" (Jung, *Psychology and Alchemy* 132) and hence not only to Christ, the quadripartite "unitary being who existed before man" and who represents "man's wholeness" (162), but also to "the unity of the Spirit [of Christ]" that exists within the undivided believer himself (Andrew Murray, *The Spirit of Christ* [Pennsylvania: Whitaker House, n.d.] 234). *Chain-Linked*

Both Self and shaman: kobold in the vein: In an ancient East Siberian legend, "The shaman [a holy man with supernatural powers] climbs the magic tree in order to find his true self in the upper world" (Jung, *Alchemical Studies* 341). See also the note on *metals* given below. *Light of the Eye*

brane: the visible, four-dimensional universe—length, width, and depth + time—contained in a higher-dimensional space, the latter membrane called "the bulk" and known as "hyperspace." *Evangelist*

breath-soul: the subtle body that—according to the alchemists—represents a concept higher than spirit (Jung, *Alchemical Studies* 213). *Fabricator; Rite*

breccias: fragmented rocks that "make up a significant portion of the [lunar] regolith and add to its complexity." Above the original bedrock, "Remotely sensed X-ray fluorescence, infrared spectra, and gamma-ray signals come from the very top of the lunar regolith [. . .]." See David S. McKay et al, "The Lunar Regolith," in *The Lunar Sourcebook—A User's Guide to the Moon*, ed. Grant H. Heiken, David Vaniman, and Bevan M. French (Cambridge: Cambridge UP, 1991) 285-86 <lpi.www.usra.edu>books> lunar_sourcebook>pdf>chapter07>. *The Man in the Moon*

A broth; then a template: See Carl Sagan, *The Cosmic Connection: An Extraterrestrial Perspective* (New York: Anchor-Doubleday, 1973). In Sagan's "scientific fable," after the titanic explosion of the Big Bang, and after the "warm, dilute broth" of the oceans had formed, "in this broth there one day arose a molecule able crudely to make copies of itself—a molecule which weakly guided the chemical processes in its vicinity to produce molecules like itself—a template molecule, a blueprint molecule, a self-replicating molecule." Soon "it gained a significant advantage over the other molecules in the early waters. The molecules that could not copy themselves did not. Those that could, did. [. . .] And then one day there came to be a creature whose genetic material was in no way different from the self-replicating molecular collectives of any of the other organisms on the planet, which he called Earth. But he was able to ponder the mystery of his origins, the strange and tortuous path by which he had emerged from star-stuff. [. . .] He was one of the starfolk. And he longed to return to the stars" (253-255). *Storyboard*

Bubble in the chaos: According to the rules of quantum logic, "whole universes, little bubbles of space-time, could pop into existence, like bubbles of boiling water, out of [. . .] nothing." See Dennis Overbye, "There's More to Nothing Than We Knew," *The New York Times* 21 Feb. 2012: 3 <www.nytimes.com>. *The Cusp of Skill; Fabricator*

Buckets the hierophant; [. . .] / Pours from Her vessel even as She scrolls: See the note on *Pours into the mill in the form of scrolls* given below. *The Woman in the Moon*

the bulk: higher-dimensional space, the cosmic membrane also known as "hyperspace." *Bootstrap; Chain-Linked; Containment and the Cosmic Edge; Fabricator*

bulk and air: i.e., hyperspace and, in the gnosis of Simon Magus, a "physicistic" conundrum: the spiritual sphere "'without beginning or end'" that contains "'a Father who upholds all things and nourishes that which has beginning and end'" (Jung, *Mysterium Coniunctionis* 136-37). *Fabricator*

bunting: a "baby's garment of soft, warm cloth made into a kind of hooded blanket that can be closed, exposing only the face" ("Bunting[1]" [n.], def. 3). See *Webster's New World Dictionary,* 1988 ed.; unless otherwise indicated, subsequent definitions of key words are from this text. *Fixated on Mars*

By beasts, and birds, and things that creep perplexed: Cf. Hos. 2.18: "Then I will make a covenant on behalf of Israel with the wild beasts, the birds of the air, and the things that creep on the earth, and I will break bow and sword and weapon of war and sweep them off the earth, so that all living creatures may lie down without fear." *Courtship*

Caelum: in alchemical texts, either "the celestial substance hidden in man" or "the kingdom of heaven upon earth" (Jung, *Mysterium Coniunctionis* 487). *The Water That Does Not Make the Hands Wet*

calèche: here, a solar *calèche* (kuh-LESH), a metonym for Christ as sun-god. A *calèche* or a calash is "a light, low-wheeled carriage, usually with a folding top" ("Calash" [n.], def. 1). *Evangelist; The Man in the Moon*

Cartesian its stem: The speaker focuses on "the kinematics of the biped robot" and "the Cartesian positions of each joint." See Juan E. Machado, Héctor M. Becerra, and Mónica Moreno Rocha, "Modeling and Finite-Time Walking Control of a Biped Robot with Feet," *Mathematical Problems in Engineering* 16 Nov. 2015: 39 <hindawi.com>. *Chain-Linked*

Castor: In Greek and Roman myth, *Castor,* the mortal twin of the immortal Pollux, represents the hyphenated God-man, since he lives half of each year on earth and half in heaven. *Circumambient; Rite; Scion; Scout; The Spear of Archytas*

A cat in a box may live or not live: See the note on *Schrödinger's Cat* given below. *Schrödinger's Cat*

The Cat's Eye Nebula: A "small blue-green blob" that the astronomer William Herschel found "in the constellation Draco the Dragon in 1786," NGC 6543 [its designated name] "is seen to have a beautiful but baffling complex structure of intersecting ovals and spirals. [. . .] Moreover, the outside of the Cat's Eye presents a series of concentric rings. Their perfectly even spacing makes astronomers conclude that, before the central star's planetary nebula erupted a mere 1,000 years ago, it emitted burps that must have created spherical shells at regular intervals. Theory cannot explain such an evenly timed choreography of eruptions, like backfires on an engine trying to start, and yet there they are. [. . .] As Nobel physicist Isidor Rabi once famously said: 'Who ordered that?'" See Bob Berman, "Weird Object: The Cat's Eye Nebula," *Astronomy* 31 July 2015: 1-7 <https://astronomy.com/magazine/weirdest-objects>, along with the definition of *nebulae* in the note given below. *Cat's Eye*

caul: the amniotic membrane that encloses a foetus. *The Heavenly Journey of the Shaman*

Cedar, pine, and cypress: According to C. G. Jung, "Numerous myths say that human beings came from trees, and many of them tell how the hero was enclosed in the maternal tree-trunk, like the dead Osiris [the Egyptian king] in the cedar-tree." In fact, countless "female deities were worshipped in tree form, and this led to the cult of sacred groves and trees. Hence when Attis [the consort of the goddess Cybele] castrated himself under a pine-tree, he did so because the tree has a maternal significance" (*Symbols of Transformation: An Analysis of the Prelude to a Case of Schizophrenia,* trans. R. F. C. Hull [1956; New York: Princeton UP, 1990] 219). Elsewhere, Jung notes that the *cypress,* a designated tree of life, is also a feminine symbol. See *Psychology and Alchemy* 72: "The Virgin Mary surrounded by her attributes," a pertinent "17th-century devotional picture." *Scintilla's Scan*

Centaurus A: Discovered in 1826 by the Scottish astronomer James Dunlop, *Centaurus A* is "a giant elliptical galaxy [in the southern constellation of *Centaurus,* the Centaur] currently in the process of devouring a [smaller] dusty barred spiral galaxy." See *Constellation Guide: Centaurus A* 12 Oct. 2014: 4 <www.constellation-guide.com/centaurus-a>. *Courtship*

Center *and* circumference; bean in the bin: In "Circles," Ralph Waldo Emerson reminds us that "St. Augustine described the nature of God as a circle whose centre was everywhere and its circumference nowhere." Later, Emerson remarks that "There is no outside, no inclosing wall, no circumference to us." In other words, each individual extends the outline of his own sphere of being (*Emerson's Esssays,* introd. Irwin Edman [1926; New York: Harper, 1951] 212, 215.) In the poem, the *bean in the bin* is the embryo developing in the womb. See Sheila Kitzinger and Lennart Nilsson, *Being Born* (New York: Grosset, 1986) 22: "You didn't look much like a baby yet— / more like a sprouting bean. . . ." *Scout*

Cepheid: "any of a class of pulsating, yellow, supergiant stars whose brightness varies in regular periods: from the period-luminosity relation, the distance of such a star can be determined" ("Cepheid [variable]" [n.], def.). *Courtship*

Cerberus: in ancient Greek literature, "the three-headed, dragon-tailed dog" that guards the gate to the underworld, a gruesome specter here pacified by "such coins as we toss." See Edith Hamilton, *Mythology* (1940; New York: Mentor-New American, 1942) 39. *Waxing in Luna into the Nature of the Sun*

chain-linked my alarm: With a compound verb the speaker alludes to the chain-link net that Hephaestus forged and with which he trapped Ares (Mars) and Aphrodite (Venus), alchemy's "gamonymous" lovers. Having confronted an unknown and unknowable robotic world, the deployed cyborg astronaut—Spacetime's redesigned *human* gamonymus: the hermaphroditic spouse of light and darkness—now betrays "a conscious attitude still dominated by fear of unconscious processes" (Jung, *Psychology and Alchemy* 217). See also

Leslie Mullen, "Cyborg Astronaut Space Race Heats Up," *Space* 8 Apr. 2010 <www.space.com>, and the note on *gamonymus* given below. *Chain-Linked*

Channeling Hipparchus: The speaker would convey the significant astronomical achievements of Hipparchus (c. 190 BC – c. 120 BC)—for example, his recorded observations concerning the frequency of lunar eclipses as well as his incidental discovery of the precession of the equinoxes—but not through Ptolemy's *Almagest* (c. AD 150), the main scholarly conduit for his ideas: on the contrary, through *experienced* "archetypal patterns" instead (Jung, *Alchemical Studies* 246). *Channeling Hipparchus*

Cheshire: the eerie cat that vanishes with a grin in Lewis Carroll's *Alice's Adventures in Wonderland.* *Cosmic Dust; Schrödinger's Cat*

Cheshires that char: massive, dying stars "present gravitationally, but not optically." Called black holes, they "are beasts akin to the smile on the Cheshire cat [. . .], enormous stars that have winked out but are still there" (Sagan, *The Cosmic Connection* 263). *Cosmic Dust*

Chiliasm's (KIL-ee-az-uhmz) Four: The speaker alludes not only to "belief in the coming of the [promised] millennium" ("Chiliasm" [n.], def.), but also to an image of the total self, a psychologically quadratic figure (Jung, *Aion* 224) not unlike "the squared circle" of the crucified Christ (204), the latter icon, in Jungian texts, a symbol of *discriminated* wholeness, since it subsumes the four psychological functions: sensation and intuition; thinking and feeling. *Extract of the Macrocosm*

chiming quartz: i.e., the *chiming quartz* crystal clock, renowned for its accuracy in the precision-measurement of time. *Ephesian Symbols*

Christ on Einstein's tram: In *The Ascent of Man* (Boston: Little, 1971), J[acob] Bronowski explicates the extraordinary riddle of "relative" Time (243) with clarity and specificity. Thus, for Sir Isaac Newton, "time and space formed an absolute framework, within which the material events of the world ran their course in an imperturbable order. His is a God's eye view of the world: it looks the same to every observer, wherever he is and however he travels." By contrast, Albert Einstein's "is a man's eye view, in which what you see and what I see is relative to each of us, that is, to our place and speed. And this relativity cannot be removed." In other words, "I in my tram and you in your chair can share no divine and instant view of events—we can only communicate our own views to one another." Furthermore, "communication is not instant," because "we cannot remove from it the basic time-lag of all signals, which is set by the speed of light" (249, 252). Nevertheless, in the last stanza of this poem, the speaker implies that Revelation's chosen believer-priests can resolve the paradox of "flexible, elastic time" (Paul Davies, *Other Worlds: A Portrait of Nature in Rebellion / Space, Superspace and the Quantum Universe* [New York: Simon, 1982] 42)— even as the historic Jesus did—when they "learn to bow to the Spirit where God dwells" (191): that is to say, in the "hidden laboratory of the inner life" (*The Spirit of Christ* 159). *Christ on Einstein's Tram*

chromosphere: "the pinkish, glowing region around a star, esp[ecially] the sun, between the hot, dense photosphere and the much hotter, tenuous corona" ("Chromosphere" [n.], def.). *A Host-Star in Draco*

Chryse: i.e., Chryse (KRY-see) Planitia (pluh-NISH-uh), a plain on Mars, the landing site of the Viking 1 spacecraft. See "Viking 1 and 2," *NASA Mars Exploration Program* 1-2 <www.mars.nasa.gov>: In 1976, "NASA's Viking Project found a place in history when it became the first U.S. mission to land a spacecraft on the surface of Mars and return images of the surface. Two identical spacecraft, each consisting of a lander and an orbiter, were built. Each orbiter-lander pair flew together and entered Mars' orbit; the landers then separated and descended to the planet's surface. The Viking 1 lander touched down on the western slope of Chryse Planitia (the Plain of Gold), while the Viking 2 lander settled down on Utopia Planitia." Thereafter, "Besides taking photographs and collecting other science data on the Martian surface, the two landers conducted three biology experiments designed to look for possible signs of life." Accessed on 14 Jan. 2020. *Drilling on Mars*

chthonic (THON-ik): "dark, primitive, and mysterious" ("Chthonic" [adj.], def. 2) and also "concrete and earthy" (Jung, *Psychology and Alchemy* 175, 177)—here, like evolving humanoid robots and even "unknown regions of the psyche" (335). *Ephesian Symbols; Local Bubble*

A circle, a spiral, a shroud that hints: a succession of numinous symbols—not only of the immutable godhead (Jean Chevalier and Alain Gheerbrant, *The Penguin Dictionary of Symbols,* trans. John Buchanan-Brown [1969; New York: Penguin, 1996] 195) and of the fertile Moon (907), but also of the evidential Resurrection of Jesus. For an update on the radiated double-body image of the crucified Savior on His burial cloth, see Gary Habermas, "The Shroud of Turin and its Significance for Biblical Studies," *Journal of the Evangelical Theological Society* (March 1981) 53 <core.ac.uk>. *Spacetime's Wight*

The circle divides; quaternal its rays— / The ground-plan of the Self—the opus plays / Like a floating isle or Theseus' maze: a hypothetical description of the alchemical *opus* as a chariot. Thus, "one's given personality could be represented by a continuous circle, whereas the conscious personality would be a circle divided up in a definite way, and this generally turns out to be a quaternity. The quaternity of basic functions [thinking, feeling, sensing, and intuiting] meets this requirement. It is therefore only to be expected that the chariot should have four wheels to correspond with the four elements or natures." In other words, "The chariot as a spherical vessel and as consciousness rests on the four elements or basic functions, just as the floating island where Apollo was born, Delos, rested on the four supports which Poseidon made for it. The wheels, naturally, are on the outside of the chariot and are its motor organs, just as the functions of consciousness facilitate the relation of the psyche to its environment. [. . .] The 'chariot of Aristotle' [a recipe "Written of old and gathered together by a certain Christian Philosopher" in the "Tractatus Aristotelis ad Alexandrum Magnum"] can be understood in this sense as a symbol of the self" (Jung, *Mysterium Coniunctionis* 201-02n478, 203). Elsewhere, Jung notes that the Theseus' myth, in which the hero journeys to the underworld in order to abduct Persephone, is also a representation of the individuation process (Jung, *Symbols of Transformation* 293n56).

However, in that tale, Theseus had to be rescued by Heracles, "the death-conquering hero," because unconsciously he "remained stuck in the mother" [i.e., "the subterranean kingdom"] and was "lost to the upper world" (292). *The Chariot of Aristotle's Wheels*

Circumambient, like His cosmic eye, / [. . .] still I ply: With these words the speaker characterizes himself as a spiritual body, the transcendental self posited, tabernacled, and indwelt by God. See Jung, *Aion* 167-68: "like every archetype, the self cannot be localized in an individual ego-consciousness, but acts like a circumambient [or surrounding] atmosphere to which no limits can be set, either in space or in time." In sum, "the self, as a content of the unconscious, is made conscious and 'fixed' [or implanted] in the mind" (168-69) by an "absolute," all-encompassing God (143). *Splitting the Earth with a Straight Foot*

Circumambient, the *opus* proceeds: See Jung, *Aion* 264-65: "The alchemists were fond of picturing their *opus* [the redemptive work of individuation] as a circulatory process"—i.e., as "the 'circular distillation' which [. . .] must be repeated a thousand times." See also the note on *Circumambient, like His cosmic eye, / [. . .] still I ply* given above. *Circumambient*

cislunar: located between Earth and the moon. In alchemical tracts, "the moon stands on the border-line between the eternal, aethereal things and the ephemeral phenomena of the earthly, sublunar realm" (Jung, *Mysterium Coniunctionis* 145). *The Chariot of Aristotle's Wheels; The Cusp of Skill; Light of the Eye; The Smoke-Hole of the Tent*

Clotho: In Greek and Roman mythology, *Clotho,* one of three Fates, spins the thread of life that Lachesis measures and that Atropos cuts. *Drilling on Mars; A Methane Snow; Psalter; Rebis; Splitting the Earth with a Straight Foot*

Clotho's thrum: the short end thread left on *Clotho's* loom after Lachesis has measured the strands and Atropos has cut and knotted them. *Local Bubble; Storyboard*

Cloverleaf: a quasar—or a *quas*(i-stell)*ar* radio source—discovered in 1988. Quasars "are thought to be the ancient, exploding origins of new galaxies and are possibly the most distant and oldest observable objects in the universe" ("Quasar" [n.], def.] *Courtship*

Cluster swallows cluster: Astronomers have discovered that "galaxies grow by swallowing smaller galaxies" and that, in fact, the giant elliptical galaxy Messier 87 (M87) merged with "an entire medium-sized [spiral] galaxy over the last billion years." See "M87 has swallowed an entire galaxy in the last billion years," *Astronomy Now* 26 June 2015: 2 <www.astronomy.com>. *Rite*

Coal Sack: either of two overlapping dust clouds in the Milky Way, especially one located near Crux, the Southern Cross, a small constellation near the South Celestial Pole. *Courtship*

Coheir's silicone sole: an image that captures the footprint left in the lunar soil at Tranquility Base — specifically, "the blue silicone sole of the lunar overshoe" designed by Richard Ellis, "a model maker" for ILC Industries, and worn by the NASA astronaut Eugene Cernan during the Apollo 17 mission. See John Branch, "One Small Step for Man, One Big Step for Moon Boots," *The New York Times* 17 July 2019: 2 <nytimes.com>. (In this line, the speaker emphasizes Photo 8 from an insert-essay—"Boot, Left, Lunar Overshoe, Cernan, Apollo 17, Flown" <airandspace.si.edu>—given in Branch's "One Small Step . . ." 5). See also the note on *Or blue silicone sole* and on *Or rungs of a ladder,* variant elliptical similes, given below. *Christ on Einstein's Tram*

coin in the roll: The *coin,* the "uncomely" metal "thrown out into the street" and rejected because of its outward "banality," is, paradoxically, a symbol of the holistic "Self" (Jung, *Psychology and Alchemy* 80-81), a goal identified in this poem as the *puer aeternus* (line 16), a Gnostic "analogy of Christ" (425). *A Methane Snow*

the collarbone of the One: a transcendental concept, "In its [funereal] mound" a symbol that appropriates the divine reality. Thus, the Dogon people of Mali, in West Africa, "regard the clavicle, or collarbone, [and] the skull, as the first [mysteria] formed by the foetus, since they support the skeleton as a whole." In fact, "Such is the importance given to clavicles by the Dogon that they place them among the five elements constituting the human personality, along with the body, the twin male and female souls, the light which these souls shed in the darkness, and the life force which they look upon as a fluid associated with the blood" (Chevalier and Gheerbrant, *The Penguin Dictionary of Symbols* 205). *Cat's Eye*

Complicit, we crown an archaic king: In this stanza, the speaker narratizes "the ritual slaying of the king," who is killed "in order to improve the condition of his people, just as God is sacrificed [in the Christian Mass: the New and Eternal Covenant] for the salvation of [hu]mankind" (C. G. Jung, *Psychology and Western Religion,* trans. R. F. C. Hull [Princeton: Princeton UP, 1984] 165). *Scintilla's Scan*

cone: a light *cone,* "the wall of light that separates our reality and other realities." In effect, "All light beams coming from a given point move along the light cone" (Bob Toben, "in conversation with" Jack Sarfatti and Fred Wolf, *Space-Time and Beyond: Toward an Explanation of the Unexplainable* [New York: Dutton, 1975] 28). *Christ on Einstein's Tram*

Conjure the wingèd soul out of its urn: Through the power of imagination, the speaker, like an alchemist, seeks to extract the compensatory "subtle body"—"a body that [is] at the same time spirit"—out of the depths of the unconscious. See Jung, *Psychology and Alchemy* 278-79, including fig. 139: "Hermes conjuring the winged soul out of an urn," and also 427-28. *Psalter*

Containment and the Cosmic Edge: The cosmologist Edward Harrison examines these "majestic" concepts in *Cosmology: The Science of the Universe,* 2nd ed. (1981; Cambridge: Cambridge UP, 2000) 147-49: "The containment principle of the physical universe states: *the physical universe contains everything that is physical and nothing else.* It is the battle cry of the physical sciences (chemistry and physics)." In other words, "Modern scientific cosmology includes all that is physical and excludes all that is nonphysical." Thus, "It includes all things that are measurable and are related by concepts that are vulnerable to disproof. Atoms and galaxies, cells and stars, organisms and planets are physical things that belong to the physical world. Particles and their corpuscular-wavelike duality, atoms and their choreography of electron waves, DNA and its genetic coding, fields and waves that propagate through space, the rich virtual worlds of the vacuum, the special relativity properties of spacetime, the general relativity properties of curved and dynamic spacetime, and the vast astronomical universe are all things of a physical nature." Harrison adds that "You cannot extend our space and time to include heaven, for heaven would then be brought into the physical universe and its existence exposed to the critical methods of scientific inquiry." Of course, Harrison realizes that "Some people will protest that the containment principle leaves out all that is most valuable. What about our souls, our minds, consciousness, and all the richness of the inner mental world, where do they fit in?" Harrison asserts that "they do not fit in anywhere. At best only their physical counterparts (such as chemical activities) fit in. All the joys of life are no more than the biochemistry of neurons in the brain. In response to those who protest and want it all put together neatly in a spiritual-psychical-physical universe, we must answer, 'You are confusing the Universe with universe. The unknown Universe is everything, including our minds; the known physical universe contains what is physical, including our brains. Mathematicians, physicists, biophysicists, and chemists have made the physical universe, and if you do not like it, despite its extraordinary success, you must make your own universe.'" Ironically, the self-inclusive speaker in this poem, having weighed the legitimacy of Harrison's reductionist perspective, and being equally aware of the incongruities and complexities of the problem, retorts with a conundrum: "each spark and each limb, / The parts of the body behind the scrim, / All the souls of the world, [are] contained in Him" (lines 22-24). For Harrison's analysis of "the cosmic-edge riddle," see the note on *Spears that vanish* given below. *Containment and the Cosmic Edge*

A continuum real in its own right: See Harrison, *Cosmology: The Science of the Universe* 147: "Space and time are not just voids into which the universe has been dropped; if they were, we could escape by searching out places in space and time not occupied by the universe. But spacetime, which is the four-dimensional physical combination of space and time, is not a mere receptacle; it is a physically real continuum. A continuum that is real in its own right." *Containment and the Cosmic Edge*

A convoy like clusters that sliding slur: The speaker refers to a quartet of elliptical galaxies that lie five billion light years away "at the centre of a galactic cluster known as CL0958+4702" and that, pulling toward one another, will eventually merge (Maggie Mckee, "Largest merger of galaxies discovered," *New Scientist* 6 Aug. 2007: 4 <www.newscientist.com>). See also the note on *Cluster swallows cluster* given above. *Storyboard*

Corpus mysticum: the Mystical Body of Christ—His united, "Pentecostal" Church (Murray, *The Spirit of Christ* 54-55). See also Jung, *Alchemical Studies* 104n8: "'Spirit' in alchemy means anything volatile, all evaporable substances, oxides, etc., but also, as a projected psychic content, a *corpus mysticum* in the sense of a 'subtle [i.e., an ethereal or a heavenly] body.'" *Here Be Dragons*

The cortex bulges; its frontal lobe furled: See Virginia Fernández, Cristina Llinares-Benadero, and Vincent Borrell, "Cerebral cortex expansion and folding: what have we learned?" *The EMBO Journal* 7 (Apr. 2016) 2 <ncbi.nlm.nih.gov>: In their study of the human brain, these authors emphasize both "the fabulous size of the cerebral cortex and its folding, visible as bulges and grooves on its external surface." In fact, cortical folding, like cortical expansion, "is of key importance for the optimization of brain wiring and functional organization." *Light of the Eye*

The cortex shambles [. . .], bootstraps the din: See Erich Harth, *Windows on the Mind: Reflections on the Physical Basis of Consciousness* (New York: Morrow, 1982) 117-18: "Comparisons between brains and computers are often misleading, but the loading of the bootstrap [the initial set of instructions that renders the computer operative] is probably a good analogue to the transformations that take place in the human brain. In the case of the brain, however, it is often difficult to say how much is built-in design and how much the bootstrap of early experience." *Bootstrap*

The cosmos stretches: recursive as sheets, / Unfolds into Gaea: In a computer game invented by John Conway in 1970 and explicated in the book *The Recursive Universe* by William Poundstone in 1985, "Everything that happens in the Life universe is strictly deterministic: the pattern at each step is completely determined by the pattern at the preceding step" and is thus *recursive,* or self-referential, like the perceiving human brain itself. In fact, "The initial pattern [. . .] fixes everything to come, *ad infinitum.* In this respect the Life universe resembles the Newtonian clockwork universe" (Paul Davies, *The Mind of God: The Scientific Basis for a Rational World* (New York: Simon, 1992) 110-11. *Storyboard*

crèche: "a display of a stable with figures, as at Christmas, representing a scene at the birth of Jesus" ("Crèche" [n.], def. 1). *Evangelist; The Man in the Moon*

a creed: i.e., the Apostles' Creed, which identifies the past, present, and future disciples of Christ—including the speaker—as a "community of saints." *Extract of the Macrocosm*

Cross-beams' quaternity: See *Aion* 224n7, where Jung remarks that "The circle has the character of wholeness because of its 'perfect' form; the quaternity, because four is the minimum number of parts into which the circle may naturally be divided." Thus, "the quaternity of Christ [. . .] is exemplified by the cross symbol" (204)—in this line, by the crossbeam attached to the vertical beam. Still, at this point in the poem, the speaker responds to an unexpected embodiment of the God-image: the astronaut himself portrayed as coheir of Christ. (See also the note below on the phrase *or else a pair.*) *The Heavenly Journey of the Shaman*

The crown of the head: here, the topmost part of the skull or *head,* i.e., in Vedic philosophy, "the point through which the soul escapes the confines of the body in order to ascend to superhuman states" (Chevalier and Gheerbrant, *The Penguin Dictionary of Symbols* 263). *The Smoke-Hole of the Tent*

Crystalline prisms: in this poem, pointed *prisms* of quartz found in geodes, each globular stone "having a cavity lined with inward growing crystals or layers of silica" ("Geode" [n.], def. 1). *The Cusp of Skill*

crystals flung from the vault of the sky: See Jung, *Mysterium Coniunctionis* 101: "In shamanism, much importance is attached to crystals, which play the part of ministering spirits. They come from the throne of the supreme being or from the vault of the sky. They show what is going on in the world and what is happening to the souls of the sick, and they also give man the power to fly." *Splitting the Earth with a Straight Foot*

CubeSats: tiny satellites designed to undertake planetary exploration. Thus, "Besides infiltrating Saturn's rings, swarms of CubeSats could fan out and explore hundreds of near-Earth asteroids, or create a network to observe electrical storms on Mars, or view regions on the sun not visible from Earth." See Mark Betancourt, "CubeSats to the Moon (Mars and Saturn, Too)," *Air&Space Magazine* Sept. 2014: 2 <www.airspacemag.com>. *Chain-Linked; Drilling on Mars*

cuboids: A cuboid is "a three-dimensional space" that allows us "to move in six directions: Left, Right, Forward, Backwards, Up and Down. This is the universe [which] we are familiar with" ("Of Hidden Dimensions and Intergalactic Space Travel," *fuzzlabs* 2 <fuzzlabs.wordpress.com>. Accessed on 1 Jan. 2015). See also Gary Weise, *The Origin of Space, Stars, Planets, and Life* (Pittsburgh, PA: RoseDog Books, 2009) 112: "Mathematics is cuboid logic, which cannot do more than an approximation of the actual geometry of the actual universe." *Channeling Hipparchus; Containment and the Cosmic Edge*

cyborg: "a hypothetical human being modified for life in a hostile or alien environment by the substitution of artificial organs or other body parts" ("Cyborg" [n.], def.). *Christ on Einstein's Tram; Evangelist; The Heavenly Journey of the Shaman*

dactyls: phallic dwarf gods, each "wonder-worker" the size of a thumb (Jung, *Symbols of Transformation* 124, 126, 127n14). According to Jung, the Idaean *dactyls* "were the first Wise Men, teachers of Orpheus, and it was they who invented the Ephesian magic formulae" (127), powerful words that supposedly conferred upon people who employed them supernatural powers. See also Michael Immendörfer, *Ephesians and Artemis: The Cult of the Great Goddess of Ephesus as the Epistle's Context* (Tübingen, Germany: Mohr Siebeck, 2017) 113. (Another aspect of the *dactyls* surfaces in the note on *Tall as a dactyl* given below.) *Ephesian Symbols; A Methane Snow*

D-brane: a concept named after the mathematician Johann Dirichlet (1805–1859)—dimensional space into which energy can flow once it leaves its quantum string. In brane cosmology, since elementary particles are thought to be neither more nor less than vibrational states of quantum strings, conservation of energy demands that each open string must have its unjoined endpoint attached to a *D-brane*. In *The Elegant Universe: Superstrings, Hidden Dimensions, and the Quest for the Ultimate Theory* (New York: Vintage-Random, 1999), Brian Greene clarifies the term even further; thus, a brane is "Any of the extended objects that arise in string theory. A one-brane is a string, a two-brane is a membrane, a three-brane has three extended dimensions" (414), and so on "up to nine-branes" (316). *A Methane Snow*

Detached from Himself and all His traces, / Jesus basks in her ointment. — As she nears, / [. . .] Toward the foetal life of His tomb He steers: See Chapter VII: "The Ointment of Bethany," in Françoise Dolto and Gérard Séverin, *The Jesus of Psychoanalysis: A Freudian Interpretation of the Gospel,* trans. Helen Lane (New York: Doubleday, 1979): In the New Testament, "There are two stories about ointment poured out on Christ [. . .] one in the Gospel of John [12.1-8] and one in the Gospel of Luke [7.36-50], but with this difference: "In John, Mary is the sister of Lazarus. In Luke, Mary is not the sister of Lazarus, but a woman of easy virtue." Nevertheless, in Luke as well as in John, each woman declares her love through her "gesture": the application of the ointment in which Jesus "basks." Thus, "Jesus accepts the homage of their feeling as [the choice of] women who, out of love, risk the criticism of others." However, in the Gospel of John, when Jesus defends the sister of Lazarus against Judas Iscariot's objection—"'Leave her alone; she had to keep this scent for the day of my burial'"—Françoise Dolto suggests that "It is precisely by these words that Jesus brings about a rupture between himself and Mary. She eroticizes her homage, and Jesus replies that he is elsewhere." In other words, "Perhaps without realizing it herself, Mary reveals his approaching death to him," with her ointment (142-43). *The Jesus of Psychoanalysis*

Devotion, Knowledge, and Love alone save: In his "Speculativa philosophia," the 16th-century Belgian alchemist Gerhard Dorn counsels the "earthly and uncleanly" artifex in the following way: "'Thou wilt never make from others the One which thou seekest, except first there be made one thing of thyself.'" Elsewhere, in "Physica Trithemii," Dorn encapsules the stages of the alchemist's spiritual ascent, succinctly, in the Church's heaven-sent triad: "'(1) devotion to the faith, (2) knowledge of God by faith, [and] (3) love from the knowledge of God'" (qtd. in Jung, *Mysterium Coniunctionis* 221n555). *Waxing in Luna into the Nature of the Sun*

diadem in the ball: The speaker refers to the auspicious caul, or amniotic membrane, of the foetus (in line 3) curled like a *ball* in the womb. For the specific source, see William Jones, *Credulities Past and Present* (1880; Detroit: Singing Tree Press, 1968): "The superstition respecting the caul is from remote antiquity, and was prevalent in the days of the Roman empire." Thus, "Aelius Lampridius in his life of Antonine, surnamed Diadumenianus, says that he was so-called from having been brought into the world with a band of membrane round his forehead, in the shape of a diadem, and that he enjoyed a perpetual state of felicity from this circumstance during the whole of his life and reign" (112). *A Methane Snow*

distal: in anatomy, a word "formed in contrast" to *proximal:* "farthest from the center or the point of attachment of origin," i.e., distant or "terminal" ("Distal" [adj.], def.). *Scion*

dot: In alchemy, the iota or indivisible point, an emblem of the holistic self, "is simple, indestructible, and eternal" (Jung, *Alchemical Studies* 186). See also Jung, *Mysterium Coniunctionis* 44n24: "The iota, the smallest Greek character," corresponds "to our 'dot' (which did not exist in Greek)." *The Heavenly Journey of the Shaman; The Smoke-Hole of the Tent*

A dragon arises: in the *opus circulatorium*, the mercurial serpent, both "an image of the sun's course" and "the substance to be transformed" (Jung, *Psychology and Alchemy* 381-82). As Jung demonstrates, "Time and again the alchemists reiterate that the *opus* proceeds from the one and leads back to the one, that it is a sort of circle like a dragon biting its own tail [. . .]. For this reason the *opus* was often called *circulare* (circular) or else *rota* (the wheel) [. . .]." In other words, the hermaphroditic Mercurius, "the world-creating spirit concealed or imprisoned in matter," appears "at the beginning and end of the work: as dragon he devours himself and as dragon he dies, to rise again as the *lapis*" (293), the radiant stone, "a symbol uniting all opposites" (295). *Mastermind*

The dragon of Babel: "the human-headed serpent of Paradise, which had the 'imago et similitudo Dei' in its head, this being the deeper reason why [in alchemical texts] the dragon devours its hated body" (Jung, *Mysterium Coniunctionis* 117). Here, of course, the *dragon* is, symbolically, but a tainted son of the first Adam redeemed by Christ. *Here Be Dragons*

the Dragon steers: See Engelbrektson, *Stars, Planets, and Galaxies* 39: Among the northern circumpolar stars, between Ursa Major (the Great Bear) and Ursa Minor (the Little Bear), lies the tail of Draco, the *Dragon*. "The remainder of the constellation curves around the bowl of the Little Dipper toward Polaris. Then the body of the Dragon curves away back in the direction of the Big Dipper's handle. Halfway back to Alkaid, in the Big Dipper, the Dragon terminates with four stars forming its head," while "other faint stars represent its fiery tongue." See the equally pertinent note on *A dragon arises* given above. *Rite*

Earthshine: See Engelbrektson, *Stars, Planets, and Galaxies* 60: "Two days after new phase, the moon is said to be a two-day-old waxing (increasing) crescent. At this time the light from the bright dayside of the earth falls on the dark nightside of the moon, and the entire face of the moon shines with a soft ashen glow called 'earthshine.'" *The Man in the Moon*

Eastward he steps: When he offers Mass *Ad Orientem*, the Roman Catholic priest either faces east or at least symbolically positions himself toward the East because, historically, Christian symbolism has connected the east with the *parousia*, the return of Christ at endtime. Thus, Jesus says, "'Like lightning from the east, flashing as far as the west, will be the coming of the Son of Man'" (Matt. 24.27). See Father John Jirak, "Ad Orientem," *Church of the Magdalen* 2-3 <www.magdalenwichita.com>. Accessed 02/14/21. *Rite*

ejecta's slough [SLUFF] / Like seas of basalts [BAY-salts]: on the Earth's moon, "vast dark plains [. . .] formed by basalts [basaltic rocks, the lava flow] from volcanic eruptions" (Denilso Camargo, "Lunar Maria," *Serious Science* 9 Sept. 2016: 3 <www.serious-science.org>). *Scout*

Elias His wheel: the chariot of fire that carried the Hebrew prophet *Elias* (Elijah) "up in the whirlwind to Heaven" (2 Kings 2.11-12). *Here Be Dragons*

Elixir: the *Elixir* of Life, an allusion to the *prima materia* in its feminine aspect—the latter "transformative substance" viewed as either a probabilistic quantum phenomenon or a more or less elusive symbol of the unconscious itself (Jung, *Mysterium Coniunctionis* 21). *The Water That Does Not Make the Hands Wet*

Elusive as Spirit or Motion's air: The speaker compares the "hyperphysical," even "ethereal" appearance of the 21st-century NASA moonwalker to the "vapour-like nature of Mercurius" in his aerial aspect, the "spirit of life" and "air in motion" being only two of the fugitive wind god's many appelations (Jung, *Alchemical Studies* 203, 212, 215). See also Erin Mahoney, ed., "A Next Generation Spacesuit for the Artemis Generation of Astronauts," *NASA: Moon to Mars* 28 Oct. 2019: 1-5 <www.nasa.gov>, an update on NASA's new Exploration Extravehicular Mobility Unit or xEMU. *The Heavenly Journey of the Shaman*

Embodiment as level as a door: The *Embodiment* is "An astronaut" (l. 21). The *door* is Christ. See John 14.6: "'I am the way; I am the truth and I am life; no one comes to the Father except by me.'" A passage from *The Spirit of Christ* that emphasizes God's "indwelling, hidden presence" is also pertinent: "I am His temple, and, in the secret place, He sits upon His throne" (Murray 211). *Extract of the Macrocosm*

Ephesian symbols: e.g., the "beauteous," self-born phoenix (Jung, *Mysterium Coniunctionis* 290); the immortal, "eye-bespangled" peacock (291), and the "alexipharmic," Mercurial serpent as the crowned dragon (334). Some Christians believe that John the Apostle did not die at Ephesus, an ancient Greek city in Asia Minor, but ascended to Heaven like Elijah. See John 21.22: "Jesus said, 'If it should be my will that he [John the Apostle] wait until I come, what is it to you?'" *Ephesian Symbols*

The Eucharist's rift: in Holy Communion, the Breaking of the Sacred Host. See *Psychology and Western Religion,* where Jung explains that, at the Holy Sacrifice of the Mass, after the Host is split in two over the Chalice, "A small piece, the *particula,* is broken off from the left half [. . .]. The sign of the cross is made over the chalice with the *particula,* and then the priest drops it into the wine" (115). In effect, "the body, or *particula,* is steeped in wine, symbolizing spirit, and this amounts to a glorification of the body. Hence the justification for regarding the *commixtio* [the mingling of the bread and wine] as a symbol of the resurrection" (116). *The Round Dance of the Stars*

Euphrates' dram: In alchemy, "the wonderful water of the Euphrates has the property of the *aqua doctrinae,* which perfects every nature in its individuality and thus makes man whole too. It does this by giving him a kind of magnetic power by which he can attract and integrate that which belongs to him" (Jung, *Aion* 185). See also John 4.10, where Christ extols the synonymous "living water." In effect, this water is "the Word sent by God" (200). *Christ on Einstein's Tram*

Even as opposites rise in the stave: In this poem, each *stave* or stanza contains such *opposites* as Heaven and Earth, Sun and Moon, Above and Below, Spirit and Body, wave and particle. See the note on *Its binary choices even as staves* given below. *Waxing in Luna into the Nature of the Sun*

Even as the Moon or Sun that She trails / Before She transmutes and thus She bails: The speaker describes the total eclipse of the Sun, "Perhaps the most spectacular of all celestial events [. . .]. On these occasions the new moon passes in front of the sun and covers the bright disk" in the darkened sky (Engelbektson, *Stars, Planets, and Galaxies* 67). See also the note on *He surrounds Her moon with His lion's mane* given below. *Psalter*

Even as the photon, phantom its size; / Velocity without place: In *Catching the Light: The Entwined History of Light and Mind* (1993; New York: Oxford UP, 1995), Arthur Zajonc reminds us that, "As Einstein said, the speed of light plays the role of an infinitely great velocity. Light has no place, but it does have a speed and we are always separated from it by 299,792,458 meters per second," or 186,000 miles. In effect, "nothing but light can reach the speed of light" (269). *Rite*

Even Ge's shapeshifter, hidden or shown, / Gravity's planet, Earth upheaves its own: Although the Sun rises in the East and sets in the West, the Earth rotates from West to East and evinces the formation of day and night. *Scion*

everything that he needs: According to the medieval alchemists, "the androgyne 'has everything [that] it needs'" because it "is already a *complexio oppositorum*" (Jung, *Mysterium Coniunctionis* 374). *Here Be Dragons*

Exalt the spheroid: The NASA astronauts trumpet the planet Earth, an oblate *spheroid*. See Duncan Steel, *Eclipse: The Celestial Phenomenon That Changed the Course of History* (Wash., DC: Joseph Henry, 2011) 51: Although it is often assumed that the Earth, Moon, and Sun are spherical, "In reality, because of their rotational properties they are each slightly flattened into shapes known as oblate spheroids, the northern hemisphere [being] a little thinner than the southern [. . .]." *The Smoke-Hole of the Tent*

Extract of the Macrocosm: See Jung, *Aion* 163n41: "The alchemist and mystic John Pordage (1607-81) called the inner 'eternal' man an 'extract [a purified form: a distilled essence] and summary concept of the Macrocosm.'" In other words, the adept knew "that as part of the whole he had an image of the whole in himself, the 'firmament' or 'Olympus,' as Paracelsus calls it." Amazingly, "This interior microcosm—["The Self beyond the Ego" (l. 18)]—was the unwitting object of alchemical research" (164). *Extract of the Microcosm*

Eye of the dome: "the 'opening' [or 'gateway to the sun'] in the CROWN of the head [. . .] through which escapes [either] the soul of the sage delivered from temporal conditions" or, according to [Lü Dongbin's Taoist masterpiece] *The Secret of the Golden Flower,* "the 'subtle' body born of the embryo of immortality" (Chevalier and Gheerbrant, *The Penguin Dictionary of Symbols* 305). See also the note on *smoke-hole of the tent* given below. *The Smoke-Hole of the Tent*

face set like a flint: Cf. Isa. 50.7-8: "I have set my face like flint, / for I know that I shall not be put to shame, / because one who will clear my name is at my side." *The Cusp of Skill*

fane: a temple or a church. *Here Be Dragons*

Fed by a crystal: i.e., by the time crystal. Posited in 2012 and identified in 2016, time crystals "look like ordinary crystals"; however, "their atoms are actually oscillating—spinning first in one direction, and then [in] the other, when exposed to an electromagnetic pulse that flips the spin." Interestingly, "Time crystals have great potential for practical applications." Thus, "They could be used to improve our current atomic clock technology—complex timepieces that keep the most accurate time that we can possibly achieve." See Michelle Starr, "Physicists Just Found Time Crystals in a Common Item You Can Buy at the Toy Store," *ScienceAlert* 3 May 2018: 2-4 <www.sciencealert.com/time-crystal-signatures-found-in-extremely-common-monoammonium-phosphate>. *Ephesian Symbols*

fettle: in Metallurgy, loose sand or crushed ore that lines the hearth of a reverberatory furnace before molten metal is poured. *Here Be Dragons*

The field of the square inch: In *Alchemical Studies,* Jung defines this mystical concept as "the symbol for that which has extension." Thus, the "central white light" of the Tao "dwells in the 'square inch' or in the face, that is, between the eyes" (25). In other words, the Savior locates His kingship in the mind of each coheir: a higher spiritual being "is invisibly born in the individual, a pneumatic body which is to serve as a future dwelling" (51-52). See also Gal. 2.20: "I have been crucified with Christ: the life I now live is not my life, but the life which Christ lives in me [. . .]." *Spacetime's Wight*

filius: in philosophical alchemy, the *filius macrocosmi,* the Son of the Macrocosm "equated with Christ." See Jung, *Alchemical Studies* 96, 126-27, and 294. *Cat's Eye*

fire that sears: either "hell-fire" or "the 'living fire' in honour of God" (Jung, *Aion* 131). *The Spear of Archytas*

Fixated on Mars I enter the ship: Dennis Overbye suggests that "Mars has always been the backyard of our imaginations, the place [where] we might one day live or from where invaders would come in flying saucers to enslave us and steal our water. Our robots have already crossed that space again and again" ("Mars Is Frigid, Rusty and Haunted. We Can't Stop Looking at It," *The New York Times*: 30 July 2018: 1 <www.nytimes.com>). See also Becky Oskin, "Why We're Obsessed with Mars," *Space.com* 5 Aug. 2012: 1-5 <www.space.com>. *Fixated on Mars*

Fixated on the world, its model cast / Even as a bubble, sintered or glassed: According to the rules of quantum logic, "whole universes, little bubbles of space-time, could pop into existence, like bubbles in boiling water, out of [. . .] nothing." See Dennis Overbye, "There's More to Nothing Than We Knew," *The New York Times* 21 Feb. 2012: 3 <www.nytimes.com>. In the poem, the artifex views each *bubble world* mock-up either as "a bonded mass of metal particles shaped and partially fused by pressure and heating below the melting point" ("Sinter" [n.], def. 2) or, simply enough, as a disc of quartz glass—a silica-based amorphous solid that has a lustrous finish when fused. *The Cusp of Skill*

foam: i.e., "the foam or sponge-like structure" of "our world canvas" (Davies, *Other Worlds* 96). See the note on *Foam in the tunnel* given below. *Rite; Storyboard*

Foam in the tunnel: With this image the speaker underscores the "sponge-like structure" of "our world canvas," the frothy fluctuations of quantum foam. See Davies, *Other Worlds* 96: "space is not uniform and featureless but, down at at [. . .] unbelievably small sizes and durations, a complex labyrinth of holes and tunnels, bubbles and webs, forming and collapsing in a restless ferment of activity." *Fabricator*

The foetus in the room—Maria's twelfth: the astrological Christ-figure—the "Son of Man"—perceived as "the first fish of the Pisces era" and as "the last ram [i.e., lamb] of the declining Aries era" (Jung, *Aion* 90). Not insignificantly, the speaker refers to the axiom of Maria Prophetissa, the storied 3rd-century alchemist, and hence to "a transformation process divided into four stages of three parts each, analogous to the twelve transformations of the zodiac and to its division into four." Thus, "the number twelve would have a not merely individual significance [as one's birth number, for instance], but a time-conditioned one, too, since the present aeon of the Fishes is drawing to its end and is at the same time the twelfth house of the zodiac" (C. G. Jung, *The Archetypes and the Collective Unconscious,* trans. R. F. C. Hull [1959; Princeton: Princeton UP, 1990] 310). In short, as Jung also indicates in *Mysterium Coniunctionis,* since the soul "was imprinted with a horoscopic character at the time of its descent into birth," the journey of each mystic traveler through the planetary houses "boils down to becoming conscious" now of one's "godlikeness" (231). See the equally pertinent note on *foetus spagyricus* and also on *Zion's cenacle* given below. *Trapeze*

foetus spagyricus: i.e., the spagyric foetus—in alchemy, the embryo of the divine child. The word *spagyric* refers to an alchemical process that both separates and combines (Jung, *Mysterium Coniunctionis* 481n91). Thus, the spagyric foetus ascends into heaven that it may become a spirit from a body and then descends to earth that it may become a body again. Cf. John 3.13: "'No one ever went up to heaven except the one who came down from heaven, the Son of Man whose home is in heaven.'" *Waxing in Luna into the Nature of the Sun*

The four-finger span and, chthonic, the thumb: the length of the forehead—hence, the brain; a variation on "the central white light" of the Tao, which "dwells in the 'square inch' or in the 'face,' that is, between the eyes" (Jung, *Alchemical Studies* 25). See the note on *The field of the square inch* given above. *Local Bubble*

From anthropoid to hierophant he stacked, / Then reconstructed an archaic fact: In the process of transformation or integration, and of illumination and hence the conscious recognition of the self, the philosophical searcher excavates "the bestial instinctive foundations of human existence," a Dionysian mystery. In effect, with the helpful intervention of both the Savior and the intellect, "the anthropoid—man as an archaic fact—is to be put together again" (Jung, *Psychology and Alchemy* 129, 131). *Claim*

From below upwards, His circle my goal / And then His temple, Ouroboros whole, / I overlap, interpenetrate, scroll, / Till I give my body back to its soul: the key passage in this poem, mainly because the speaker attempts to grasp concepts that prove as circuitous as they are ineffable. Nevertheless, citing Georg Koepgen's *Die Gnosis des Christentums* (Salzburg, 1939), Jung reminds us that "The thinking in the psalms and of the prophets is [necessarily] 'circular. Even the Apocalypse consists of spiral images.'" Indeed, to buttress his argument, Koepgen gives an example from the sainted monk Ephraem Syrus (c. 306-373): "'Make glad the body through the soul, but give the soul back to the body, that both may be glad that after the separation they are joined again.'" Jung observes that "An alchemist could have said the same of the uroboros, since this is the primal symbol of alchemical truth." Jung adds that, not insignificantly, Koepgen, a Catholic theologian, also views *dogma* [emphasis mine] as being 'circular' even as he calls attention to the "'fact of not knowing and not recognizing, which lies at the core of the dogma itself.'" Of course, as Jung notes, this remark "indicates the reason or one of the reasons for the 'roundness': dogmas are approximate concepts for a fact that exists yet cannot be described, and can only be approached by circumambulation. At the same time, these facts are 'spheres' of indeterminable extent, since they represent *principles.* Psychologically they correspond to the archetypes. Overlapping and interpenetration are an essential part of their nature. 'Roundness' is a peculiarity not only of dogmas, but, in especial degree, of alchemical thought" (*Mysterium Coniunctionis* 102-03n54). *The Water That Does Not Make the Hands Wet*

From cave to cone: an image of ascension—from "a hollow place inside the earth" ("Cave" [n.], def. 1) to the blunt nose cone on the NASA Space Shuttle's external tank. See the note on *cone* given above and the note on *Gateway* given below. *Gateway*

From oxygen and carbon we are made . . . / Sodium, iron, zinc, as Spacetime bade: the speaker's scattershot list of necessary elements found in the human body. *A Host-Star in Draco*

funnelweb: the filmy network either of the Milky Way or of the Funnelweb Mygalomorph, a "dangerously poisonous spider" that catches insects "by entangling them in a sheet of silk. The spider hides in a tube in one corner of the sheet." See Herbert W. Levi and Lorna R. Levi, *A Guide to Spiders and Their Kin* (New York: Golden-Western, 1968) 16, 24. *The Path of Least Action*

furnace: here, the mother's womb in which the speaker imagines that he gestates in order to be reborn. See Jung, *Psychology and Alchemy* 347, fig. 184, titled "The three youths in the fiery furnace," where fire symbolizes the divine presence, i.e., "the spirit concealed in matter" (346). *The Path of Least Action*

Gaea's Cenacle: "the room in which Jesus and his disciples ate the Last Supper" ("Cenacle" [n.], def.). Gaea, a variant form of Ge, is both the Greek goddess of Earth and the Supreme Mother of all life. *The Jesus of Psychoanalysis*

Gaea's swain: here, the NASA astronaut perceived as "a lover or suitor" ("Swain" [n.], def. 3), the betrothed of Spacetime. *Evangelist*

The Galilean satellites: Discovered by Galileo Galilei (1564-1642), the four largest moons of Jupiter are Io, Europa, Ganymede, and Callisto. *Gateway*

Gamonymous (guh-MAHN-uh-muss): here, the adjectival form of the Greek term "gamonymus": "having the name of matrimony" (Jung, *Mysterium Coniunctionis* 465). See the note on *gamonymus* given below. *Christ on Einstein's Tram; Evangelist; Scintilla's Scan; Scion*

gamonymus (guh-MAHN-uh-muss): In *Alchemical Studies,* Jung defines the Greek term *gamonymus* as "a kind of chymical wedding," i.e., as the sealed product of the "indissoluble, hermaphroditic union [of Sol and Luna]" (136). See also Jung, *Mysterium Coniunctionis,* where the divine pair that unite in the alchemical *opus* represent "a true 'gamonymus' in the Paracelsan sense" (485). *Local Bubble; A Methane Snow; The Spear of Archytas*

Gateway: a catchall for key ideas in this poem. See Chevalier and Gheerbrant, *The Penguin Dictionary of Symbols* 422: "Gateways symbolize the scene of passing from one state to another, from one world to another, from the known to the unknown, from light to darkness. Doors open upon the mysterious, but they have a dynamic psychological quality for they not only indicate a threshold but invite us to cross it. It is an invitation to a voyage into the beyond." Equally relevant is the Lunar Gateway, "an outpost that stays in constant orbit around the moon. The lunar gateway will be a docking hub for astronaut expeditions as they move on to their final mission, be that the lunar surface or beyond" (Trevor English, "The Lunar Gateway is NASA's Stepping Stone to Lunar Habitation," *Interesting Engineering* 10 Nov. 2020: 1 <https:/interestingengineering.com>). See also the note on *Eye of the dome* given above. *Gateway*

gegenschein **(GAY-gen-shine):** "a diffuse, faint light, sometimes visible almost directly opposite the sun in the night sky, and thought to be sunlight reflected from dust" ("Gegenschein" [n.], def.). *Cosmic Dust*

Geminga's remnant: See David Darling, "Geminga," *The World of David Darling,* n.d: 1-2 <www.daviddarling.info>: "Geminga is a neutron star in the constellation Gemini that is the second brightest source of high-energy gamma rays in the sky. Discovered in 1972 by the SAS-2 satellite, its name is both a contraction of 'Gemini gamma-ray source' and an expression in Milanese dialect meaning 'it's not there.'" Accessed 12 Sept. 2020. *Local Bubble*

Ge's conundrum: either *quid* or *quis:* In this poem, Gaea [JEE-uh], both the Greek Goddess of the Earth and the Supreme Mother of All Life, underscores, "like puzzling reflections in a mirror" (1 Cor. 13.12), "the antinomial character of the self" (Jung, *Psychology and Alchemy* 21). Thus, in the speaker's worldview, since "Christ undoubtedly represents the self" (Jung, *Aion* 62), the "distinction between 'quis' [who] and 'quid' [what] is crucial: whereas 'quis' has an unmistakably personal aspect and refers to the ego, 'quid' is neuter, predicating nothing except an object which is not even endowed with personality. Not the subjective consciousness of the psyche is meant, but the psyche itself as the unknown, unprejudiced object that still has to be investigated. The difference between knowledge of the ego and knowledge of the self could hardly be formulated more trenchantly than in this distinction between 'quis' and 'quid'" (164). *Psalter*

Ge's orb-weaver's web: the gossamer network of the universe compared to a spider's (here, an *orb-weaver's*) *web* of silk. *The Spear of Archytas*

Ge's simulated plats: various constellations of the CubeSat platform—e.g., such applications as a disposable probe dropped "into Venus's atmosphere, or onto one of Jupiter's moons," or even each of the "hexadecimal mirror segments" from the James Webb Space Telescope placed "onto its own CubeSat." See the interview with Dr. Larry Kepko, a NASA research astrophysicist, in "CubeSat/SmallSat," *NASA Goddard Tech Transfer News* 15 (2017): 9 <www.etd.gsfc.nasa.gov>, and also the note on *CubeSats* given above. *Drilling on Mars*

Gilead's balm: an aromatic ointment; hence, "anything healing or soothing" ("Balm of Gilead," def. 2). Of course, in this poem, the speaker alludes to a rhetorical question that the mournful prophet asks in Jer. 8.22: "Is there no balm in Gilead, no physician there?" Gilead is "a mountainous region of ancient Palestine, east of the Jordan" ("Gilead," def.). *Scintilla's Scan*

A girdle of shells: in a North American Indian legend, and in Longfellow's "great narrative poem, *The Song of Hiawatha*," the "magic belt of wampum," i.e., of small beads made of polished *shells,* a prize equivalent in Judaeo-Christian symbology to "the treasure hard to attain" (Jung, *Symbols of Transformation* 312, 316). *Splitting the Earth with a Straight Foot*

Globular clusters with smiles that yet jar: The speaker refers to the "supermassive black holes (many millions of times our Sun's mass) that lie at the cores of galaxies" (Lynn Jenner, ed., "Hubble Uncovers Concentration of Small Black Holes," *NASA* 11 Feb. 2021 <www.nasa.gov>). See also the note on *Cheshires that char* given above. *Cosmic Dust*

glyph: "a pictograph [a hieroglyphic] or other symbolic character or sign, esp[ecially] when cut into a surface or carved in relief" ("Glyph" [n.], def. 1). *Circumambient; The Water That Does Not Make the Hands Wet*

A glyph on a tablet: The Moon that came, / In Her stream His scion, photon or flame: As a mirror of the androgynous Original Man of Gnosticism, the masculo-feminine speaker reifies the archetype of Yahweh's sun-moon hermaphrodite, the *rebis* whose picture appears in Jung, *Psychology and Alchemy* 244, fig. 125. *Claim*

gnomon: See the photo of a *gnomon* amid the "[t]ire marks and footprints in the lunar dust in the Descartes highlands during the Apollo 16 EVA [Extra Vehicular Activity]" in Robin Kerrod, *Space Walks* (New York: Gallery-Smith, 1985) 43: "The instrument in the foreground is a gnomon. It is a device used for calibrating pictures of the surface. It provides a vertical rod of known length and a color chart." *Waxing in Luna into the Nature of the Sun*

God in the swirl, / Once perfected, it becomes like a whirl: a description of the redemptive character of alchemy. Although the speaker may be fixated at first on the material substances of the hermetic art, he ultimately seeks the salvation of the immortal inner man through the spiritual regeneration of matter. Cf. "the mystic logion" of the Greek-Egyptian alchemist Zosimos (c. AD 300) cited in Jung, *Psychology and Alchemy* 386: "And what meaneth this: 'the nature that conquers the natures,' and 'it [the transforming substance] is perfected and becometh like a whirl'?"—i.e., like "the revolving heavens [. . .] reflected in the unconscious." In short, for the alchemists, apparently "'nature' can improve or free itself from error only in and through itself" (Jung, *Aion* 143). *Mastermind*

Gog's gamonymus: a perversion of alchemy's true *gamonymus*. In Rev. 20.8, the paired kings Gog and Magog represent the satanic nations destined to war against the kingdom of God at the end of the world. See the note on *gamonymus* given above. *The Spear of Archytas*

the Goldilocks Zone: See Pat Brennan, "Goldilocks Zone," *NASA Exoplanet Exploration* 3 Mar. 2021: 1-2 <www.exoplanets.nasa.gov>: "Because our blueprint for life is Earth, astronomers look for planets with Earth-like characteristics, like liquid water. But a celestial object can only orbit so close (like Mercury) or so far (like Pluto) from its star before water on its surface boils away or freezes. The 'Goldilocks Zone,' or habitable zone, is the range of distance with the right temperatures for water to remain liquid. Discoveries in the Goldilocks Zone [. . .] are what scientists hope will lead us to water—and one day life." *A Host-Star in Draco*

the googlesphere: the universe; an absurdist coinage based on another (root) neologism. Thus, the term "googol" (*goo*-gall), which signifies "the number 1 followed by 100 zeroes" (in short, "any very large number"), derives from "the arbitrary use by E. Kasner (1878-1955), U.S. mathematician, of a child's word"—i.e., "goo" ("Googol" [n.], defs. 1, 2). In regard to the "loopy self-consistency" of the "laws of physics and computable mathematics," see Davies, *The Mind of God* 108: "The fact that the physical world reflects the computational properties of arithmetic has a profound implication." It suggests that, "in a sense, the physical world *is* a computer [. . .]." *The Path of Least Action*

Grappled Hubble with my robotic arm: In December 1993, during the first servicing mission to the Hubble Space Telescope, NASA astronauts, having used Canadarm, the shuttle's *robotic arm,* to "raise Hubble from the payload bay and out into space," successfully installed "a set of specialized lenses to correct the flawed main mirror in the telescope." See Rob Garner and Brian Dunbar, "About – Hubble Servicing Missions," *Hubble Space Telescope* 15 July 2020: 2 <www.nasa.gov>. *Chain-Linked*

the great south wind: See Jung, *Psychology and Alchemy* 387: "in the writings of the Church Fathers the south wind is an allegory of the Holy Ghost, presumably because it is hot and dry. For the same reason the process of sublimation is known in Arabic alchemy as 'the great south wind,' referring to the heating of the retort." Thus, Abu'l Qâsim remarks that "'The great south wind when it acts makes the clouds to rise [. . .] to the top of the retort'" (387n130). *Mastermind*

The Guest that banquets: At the Sabbath meal, in the house of an eminent Pharisee, Jesus "said to his host, 'When you are having a party for lunch or supper, do not invite your friends, your brothers or other relations, or your rich neighbours; they will only ask you back again and so you will be repaid. But when you give a party, ask the poor, the crippled, the lame, and the blind; and so find happiness. For they have no means of repaying you; but you will be repaid on the day when good men rise from the dead" (Luke 14.12-14). *Trapeze*

Hauled his seismometer: i.e., a seismograph, "an instrument that records the intensity and duration of earthquakes and similar tremors" ("Seismograph" [n.], def.). See also the picture of the Apollo 11 landing site in Kerrod, *Space Walks* 34, which features "some of the experimental equipment deployed by the astronauts," including "a seismometer to measure 'moonquakes.'" *Waxing in Luna into the Nature of the Sun*

having eyes yet seeing not: Jung notes that, in "Philosophia meditativa" (*Theatrum chemicum,* vol. 1 [1602] 459), the spiritual alchemist Gerhard Dorn laments that "the spark of divine fire implanted in man" is a heavenly treasure that "'the animal man understandeth not. . . . We are made like stones, having eyes and seeing not'" (*Mysterium Coniunctionis* 96). *The Water That Does Not Make the Hands Wet*

The Heavenly Journey of the Shaman: here, not only the miraculous ascension of Jesus into Heaven at the right hand of God (Acts 1.9-11), but also the rocket-borne orbital flight of the NASA astronaut to the moon and beyond. According to Jung, in the literature of the alchemists, "the climbing of the magical tree," a universal symbol of both the innermost personality and the transpersonal self, is also "the heavenly journey of the shaman, during which he encounters his heavenly spouse," i.e., his anima (*Alchemical Studies* 303), a "union of opposites" (341) that leads to the integration of the conscious and the unconscious and thereafter to the enlightened goal of the opus: the self-actualized "individuation of the adept" (326). *The Heavenly Journey of the Shaman*

Heaven's mate— / *Ge's* **coheir—implicate; wholeness its slate, / The omniverse itself predestinate:** a worldview proposed by David Bohm (1917-1994), a renowned theoretical physicist. In this model of reality—as in a hologram—any element contains, enfolded within itself, the totality of the universe. The adjective *implicate* [IM-pli-kate] derives from the Latin term *implicare,* to unite, involve, or entangle. See the note on *We enter the retort* given below. *Local Bubble*

He buckets the souls: See the note on *Jesus bucketed souls beyond the grave* given below. *Trapeze*

He combines all colors: a muted reference to the peacock, "an early Christian symbol for the Redeemer" (Jung, *Psychology and Alchemy* 419), since its "combination of all colors" signifies wholeness (223). Elsewhere, Jung notes that, in medieval literature, peacock flesh is the food of immortality (*Mysterium Coniunctionis* 292). *Mastermind*

He enters Her navel; Adam thus groined, / He swallows the nature to which he is joined: The speaker compares the foetal [second] Adam to Ouroboros, "the dragon [that] devours himself from the tail upwards until his whole body has been swallowed into his head" (Jung, *Mysterium Coniunctionis* 117). For the alchemists the mercurial dragon symbolizes the "circulatory process" that leads to life, self-fertilization, and rebirth (365). *Schrödinger's Cat*

He grasped the tiny sleeve of skin and flapped / With his instrument: The speaker describes the rite of circumcision, here not only "a milder form" of self-castration, but also "a transcendental mystery" that symbolizes both the priestly renewal of life and the ritual ransom from the fear of death (Jung, *Symbols of Transformation* 430-31). *Local Bubble*

He has spanned / The unity of the whole with His hand: In *Mysterium Coniunctionis,* Jung emphasizes the significant role that "the opposites and their union play in alchemy." Thus, "paradoxes cluster most thickly round the arcane substance," a synonym for the two-faced Mercurius, who not only contained the opposites "in uncombined form as the prima materia," but also, in his "amalgamated" conversion as the *lapis Philosophorum,* "'showed with his hand the unity of the whole,'" a mystic doctrine that the "Archpriest" Komarios supposedly taught to Cleopatra, in alchemical lore an ancient female adept (42-43). As Chevalier and Gheerbrant remind us in *The Penguin Dictionary of Symbols,* in "Old Testament and Christian traditions the hand is the symbol of [divine] power and [anointed] supremacy" (469). Not surprisingly, then, in this stanza, the speaker even refers to the Risen Christ, the thematically transposed "Bridegroom"—"Both hidden and manifest"—of John 3.29 and Rev. 19.7-9. *Fabricator*

He houses four cameras in his head; / For depth perception one more, infrared, / Mounted in his mouth: an excerpt from NASA's description of Robonaut 2, a dexterous humanoid robot designed for space travel: "Behind R2's visor are four visible light cameras—two to provide stereo vision for the robot and its operators, and two auxiliary [or backup] cameras. A fifth infrared camera is housed in the mouth area for depth perception" (*Robonaut 2: Fact Sheet* 2 <www.nasa.gov>). Accessed 10 Mar. 2022. *The Moon in Transition Raised to the Sun*

He leads His nomad to His solar tree: the *tree* conceived as a disguised symbol of the lunisolar hermaphrodite. Thus, Christ leads each wandering pilgrim either to the maternal warmth of His outstretched Cross, "'the pole of the world'" (Chevalier and Gheerbrant, *The Penguin Dictionary of Symbols* (254), or, along the same ascensional path, to the phallic power of His nursing Father (Acts 13.17). These authors emphasize that, "sexually, tree symbolism is ambivalent. The Tree of Life may originally have been regarded as an image of the primordial hermaphrodite, but on the level of the phenomenal world the trunk rising to the skies, a symbol of pre-eminently solar strength and power, is really the phallus, the archetypal image of the Father. On the other hand, the hollow tree, as well as the tree covered with thick and interwoven foliage in which birds nest and which bears an annual crop of fruit, conjures up the archetypal lunar image of the fruitful mother" (1031). *Scintilla's Scan*

heliosphere: the ever-expanding, "giant bubble carved out by the solar wind" (Miles Hatfield, "As Solar Wind Blows, Our Heliosphere Balloons," *NASA* 6 June 2018: 1 <www.nasa.gov>). Hatfield reminds us that the heliosphere "encases all the planets in our solar system and much of the space beyond them, separating the domain of our Sun from that of interstellar space" (3). *Rite*

He offends the flesh: Cf. Dolto and Sévérin, *The Jesus of Psychoanalysis* 32: "everything concerning our spiritual life is an offense to the flesh." In the poem, the speaker refers to the Risen Savior, the "higher spiritual being who is invisibly born in the individual," the incorruptible "pneumatic body which is to serve us as a future dwelling, a body which, as Paul says, is put on like a garment" (Jung, *Alchemical Studies* 52). See 1 Cor. 27: "Now you are Christ's body, and each of you a limb or organ of it." *A Methane Snow*

He opens the hatch; stands up in his seat; / [. . .] His spacesuit bulky, walks without a cleat: This verbal portrait mirrors the iconic photograph of the Shuttle astronaut Bob Stewart in Joseph P. Allen and Russell Martin, *Entering Space: An Astronaut's Odyssey* (New York: Stewart, 1984) 112. In his multi-layered spacesuit, Stewart is attached to the Manned Maneuvering Unit (MMU), a jetpack propulsion system [the "hand-held" heat of line 11] that he "latches to the hard-shell torso" of his spacesuit and operates, untethered, during the *Challenger* deployment of two communication satellites in 1984 (113). [Deemed risky, the MMU has been replaced since 1994 by the Simplified Aid for EVA Rescue (SAFER), a smaller, mobility-aiding backpack worn during spacewalks and used in case of emergency only.] Nevertheless, the MMU still evokes the image of the astronaut as "a wandering microcosm" (Jung, *Aion* 218-19), a supernal vision not unlike the primordial figures of both the *anima mundi* [the world soul] and the Original Man "hatched" from the Cosmic Egg "incubated by the Sun" (Chevalier and Gheerbrant, *The Penguin Dictionary of Symbols* 337)—in short, a God-image latent in the darkness of matter that, "because of its quaternary character and its roundness, must be regarded as a symbol of wholeness" (198). See also the note on *I opened the hatch, stood up in my seat* given below. *The Man in the Moon*

Hephaestus: in Greek literature, the lame god who presides over fire, metals, and metallurgy. In Homer's *Odyssey,* he is also the husband of Aphrodite, the Goddess of Love. *Chain-Linked; Containment and the Cosmic Edge; Here Be Dragons; Scion; Scout*

He points to the Messiah; haloed, crossed, / Reborn as the Bridegroom, His body tossed, / He infills the spheroid: See Jung, *Mysterium Coniunctionis* 35n194, where Professor Hugo Rahner offers a trenchant analysis of solar and lunar eclipses and "the *kenosis* [the emptying] of the bridegroom" in alchemical literature. "The remarkable paradox of Luna, that she is darkest when nearest the sun, is a symbol of Christian asceticism. 'The more the inward man draws nigh to the sun, the more is the outward man destroyed, but the inward man is renewed from day to day (a variation of II Cor. 4:16). That is, the Christian dies like Luna and his life is 'hid with Christ in God' (Coloss. 3:3). All this Augustine says in *Epistola* 55, v, 8.'" What it means for the theme of this poem is patent: "Just as the *kenosis* of Christ was fulfilled in death, even death on the cross (Phil. 2:8), and out of this death the 'glory' of the divine nature (2.9f.) was bestowed on Christ's 'form as a servant' (2.7), whence this whole process can be compared with the setting (death) of the sun and its rising anew (glory), [. . .] so is it with the parallel *kenosis* of Ecclesia-Luna [the Church and the Moon]" and, by extension, of the *Reborn* NASA astronaut of this opening stanza. *The Man in the Moon*

He pours from His fire like molten metal: Cf. Jung's description of the Son of Man in Rev. 1.15: "the feet stand in the fire and glow like molten metal" (Jung, *Mysterium Coniunctionis* 441). *Here Be Dragons*

Heracleian magnet: i.e., here, not Heracles (or Hercules), but Christ: the animate stone—"the magnet that draws to itself those parts or substances in man that are of divine origin [. . .] and carries them back to their heavenly birthplace" (Jung, *Aion* 185-86). *Christ on Einstein's Tram*

Heracles' car: in Greek mythology, the chariot of Heracles (or Hercules), the Sun-hero "who submits to arduous labours and to the passion of self-cremation" and sublimation "culminating in divinity" (Jung, *Psychology and Alchemy* 381, 307n36). With this prod, the speaker evokes a familiar archetype—alchemy's *corpus subtile,* "a transfigured and resurrected body, i.e., a body that [is] at the same time spirit" (427-28). *Cat's Eye*

He raked lunar rock chips: The speaker refers to "the lunar rock samples brought back to the Earth by Apollo 11" (Kerrod, *Space Walks* 35). Kerrod remarks that, although "the Moon has slightly different kinds of minerals from those on Earth, [. . .] it contains no new elements. Most lunar rocks are either volcanic, like basalt, or are composed of cemented rock chips, like breccia." *Waxing in Luna into the Nature of the Sun*

Here Be Dragons: the translation of a Latin phrase—*hic sunt dracones*—used by sixteenth-century European mapmakers to signify unknown or perilous terrain. *Here Be Dragons*

herm: "a square pillar of stone topped by a bust or head, originally of Hermes" [the Greek god of revelation, the herald and messenger of the other gods] ("Herm" [n.], def.). *Scion*

Hermaphrodite (her-*maf*-roh-dite): after Hermaphroditus, the son of Hermes and Aphrodite. While bathing, he became united in a single body with the nymph Salmacis. In *The Archetypes and the Collective Unconscious,* Jung suggests that, although "the original hermaphrodite type [. . .] seems to go far back into prehistory" (69n27), in modern psychological parlance, "The hermaphrodite means nothing less than a union of the strongest and most striking opposites. [. . .] As civilization develops, the bisexual primordial being turns into a symbol of the unity of personality, a symbol of the self, where the war of opposites finds peace. In this way the primordial being becomes the distant goal of man's self-development, having been from the beginning a projection of his unconscious wholeness" (173-75). See also *Mysterium Coniunctionis* 408: In a key passage, Jung indicates that, at the Creation, "Adam must have had two faces, in accordance with [the Rabbinic] interpretation of Psalm 139.5: 'Thou hast beset me behind and before' [. . .]." *The Water That Does Not Make the Hands Wet*

Hermes: In Greek mythology, *Hermes,* "the god who serves as herald and messenger of the other gods," is "generally pictured with wingèd shoes and hat, carrying a caduceus [. . .]" ("Hermes" [n.], def.). His Roman counterpart is Mercury. Significantly, Jung notes that, in alchemical literature, "Hermes or Mercurius possessed a double nature, being a chthonic god of revelation and also the spirit of quicksilver, for which reason he was represented as a hermaphrodite" (*Psychology and Alchemy* 65). *Bootstrap; Christ on Einstein's Tram; The Cusp of Skill; Local Bubble; The Man in the Moon; Scout; The Smoke-Hole of the Tent; The Spear of Archytas*

Hermes round and square: In alchemy, *Hermes,* god of revelation, "is associated with the idea of roundness and also of squareness, as can be seen particularly in Papyrus V (line 401) of the *Papyri Graecae Magicae,* where he is named [. . .] 'round and square,'" i.e., "a totality consisting of four parts," or four elements, like "the mysterious transforming substance" of "the Gnostic quadripartite original man" (Jung, *Psychology and Alchemy* 132-33). *The Cusp of Skill*

Hermes' syrinx: a primitive wind instrument—a shepherd's reed pipe that Hermes, the Divine Herald of the gods, invented and that Pan, Hermes' son, also made. In the latter version of the Greek myth, Pan "loved a nymph named Syrinx who fled from him and [who] just as he was about to seize her was turned [by her sister nymphs] into a tuft of reeds," plumelike grasses out of which Pan fashioned his consolatory musical instrument (Hamilton, *Mythology* 77). *Cat's Eye*

Hermes' tryst: Hermes, the herald of the gods, had seduced Aphrodite, the goddess of love, and out of their union a son, Hermaphroditus, was born. Later, while bathing, Hermaphroditus was physically united with the smitten nymph Salmacis, the two of them sealed thereafter in the Hermetic mind as Mythology's archetypal androgyne. For a detailed view of this subject, see the note on *hermaphrodite* given above. *Extract of the Macrocosm*

Hermetic: derived from Hermes Trismegistus, the first alchemist and emblematic magus. The note on *Hermes* given above is also pertinent. *Schrödinger's Cat*

He saw a crater and then a boulder: During the landing of Apollo 11, the onboard computer was taking Commander Neil Armstrong "toward the near slope of a crater the size of a football field. Later designated West Crater, it was surrounded by a large boulder field. Some of the hefty rocks in it were the size of Volkswagens." See James R. Hansen, *First Man: The Life of Neil A. Armstrong* (New York: Simon, 2005) 466. *Waxing in Luna into the Nature of the Sun.*

He sought to be neither woman nor man, / But both these sexes: a description of the *rebis,* "The dual being born of the alchemical union of opposites" (masculine/feminine) and recognized "as a symbol of the self" (Jung, *Aion* 268). See also Rabbi Mark Sameth's illuminating essay "Is God Transgender?" in *The New York Times* 13 August 2016: A17: "the Hebrew Bible, when read in its original language, offers a highly elastic view of gender. And I do mean *highly* elastic: In Genesis 3:12, Eve is referred to as 'he.' In Genesis 9:21, after the flood, Noah repairs to 'her' tent. Genesis 24:16 refers to Rebecca as a 'young man.' And Genesis 1:27 refers to Adam as 'them.' [. . .] And there are many other, even more vivid examples: In Esther 2:17, Mordecai is pictured as nursing his niece Esther. In a similar way, in Isaiah 49:23, the future kings of Israel are prophesied to be 'nursing kings.' Why would the Bible do this? These aren't typos. [The answer is that] In the ancient world, well-expressed gender fluidity was the mark of a civilized person. Such a person was considered more 'godlike.' [. . .] Counter to everything [that] we grew up believing," the God of Israel "was understood by its earliest worshippers to be a dual-gendered deity." (Even Rabbi Daniel Ross Goodman, a respondent who subsequently disagreed with the latter thesis, maintained that "Positing a transgender God is the kind of bold, imaginative thinking that we sorely need in contemporary theology" ["Gender Identity in Olden Times: Interpreting the Torah," *The New York Times* 19 August 2016: A20].) *Rebis*

He spins in the heavens: the NASA astronaut projected as the foetal form of Gaea's still-gestating race. See Jung, *Aion* 221n157: "'Jesus is still in the making.'" The original source is R. Roberts, "Jesus or Christ?—A Reply," *The Quest* 2 (London, 1911) 124. *The Heavenly Journey of the Shaman*

He stands on the round chaos; holds the scales: The speaker evokes the double image of "Mercurius as the sun-moon hermaphrodite (*rebis*), standing on the (round) chaos" (Jung, *Psychology and Alchemy* 244, fig. 125), and "Mercurius, standing on the round chaos, holding the scales which signify the *pondus et mensura* [the weights and measures]" (324, fig. 164). Elsewhere, Jung defines the idea of *the round chaos* as the primordial "life-mass," the "confused assortment of crude disordered matter" (144n59) that, containing all the elements, not only prefigures the gold, but also gives birth to the *lapis philosophorum*—the living philosophical stone (325), i.e., "the [mercurial] figure [of Christ] veiled in matter" (*Alchemical Studies* 247). *Psalter*

He stirs in the vas such Monads as brim / Even as Adam, each spark and each limb, / The parts of the body behind the scrim, / All the souls of the world, contained in him: See *Mysterium Coniunctionis* 413-14: Quoting the 16th-century Cabalist Christian Knorr von Rosenroth (from his *Kabbala Denudata*), Jung observes that, when Ezekiel 34.31 says, "'Ye are Adam,'" he means that "'all the souls of the Israelites were in truth nothing but the first-created [cosmogonic] Adam'" [Kadmon] and that "'you were his sparks and his limbs.'" In other words, according to Jung, "Adam [Kadmon] appears on the one hand as the body of the people of Israel and on the other as its 'general soul.'" However, Jung emphasizes that, in the latter passage, as the "inner" man, Adam [Kadmon] is—in the *psychological* interpretation of the subject—"the totality of the individual, the synthesis of all parts of the psyche, and therefore of the conscious and the unconscious." Jung also underscores the idea that "the saving wholeness of the inner man—i.e., the 'Messiah'—cannot come about until all parts of the psyche have been made conscious." In fact, "This [desideratum] may be sufficient to explain why it takes so long for the second Adam to appear"—not the "old Adam," but rather "the still older [androgynous and pneumatic] Adam [Kadmon] before the Fall" (452-53). (For perhaps the final word concerning the ground-plan of the totalistic self, see 1 Cor. 15.44-47: "If there is such a thing as an animal body, there is also a spiritual body. It is in this sense that Scripture says, 'The first man, Adam, became an animate being,' whereas the last Adam has become a life-giving spirit." In sum, "The first man was made 'of the dust of the earth': the second man is from heaven.") *Containment and the Cosmic Edge*

He surrounds Her Moon with His lion's mane: The speaker recalls the Sol-Luna allegory, a staple of alchemical thought. In this psychologem, the "daemonic quality which is connected with the dark side of the moon [. . .] displays its full effect." Not surprisingly, then, during the solar eclipse, Sun and Moon "reveal their antithetical nature" even as "the two opposites cancel each other out." However, in the Christian version of the Sol-Luna relationship, their "impact" results "in the birth of a third and new thing," a savior-son "who resolves the antagonisms of the parents and is himself a 'united double nature,'" i.e., New Heaven's archetypal androgyne (Jung, *Mysterium Coniunctionis* 29). See also *Aion* 91n75, where Jung asserts, not impertinently, that "In whatsoever a man is involved, there his sexuality will appear too." *Channeling Hipparchus*

He swallows his body into his head: Ouroboros, "the dragon [that] devours himself from the tail upwards until his whole body has been swallowed into his head" (Jung, *Mysterium Coniunctionis* 117). For the alchemists, the mercurial dragon symbolizes the "circulatory process" that leads to life, self-fertilization, and rebirth" (365). *Here Be Dragons*

He tinctures His remnant: The speaker knows that, in the "hidden laboratory of the inner life" (Murray, *The Spirit of Christ* 159), the Savior has imbued with Spirit His believer-priests, the heavenly *remnant* of Endtime already "ransomed as the firstfruits of humanity for God and the Lamb" (Rev. 14.3-5). See also Murray 42: "This baptism of the Holy Spirit is the crown and glory of Jesus' [redemptive] work." *Containment and the Cosmic Edge*

He touches down lightly; expands Her threads / In the Cayley Plains: This passage back-tracks from the satellite-repair-and-recovery mission in the preceding stanza—a deployment that occurred during the fourth flight of the space shuttle *Challenger* in 1984—to the Apollo 16 sampling of "lunar light plains deposits designated Cayley Formation," predominantly non-volcanic, "light-colored plagioclase-rich breccias" that NASA astronauts John Young and Charles Duke collected in 1972. See E. C. T. Chao, et al., "Lunar Light Plains Deposits (Cayley Formation)—A Reinterpretation of Origin," *Lunar and Planetary Institute* 1973: 1 <Apollo 16–Cayley Plains.pdf>. The phrase *Her threads* refers either to Gaea (l. 18), the Supreme Mother of *all* life (Anne Baring and Jules Cashford, *The Myth of the Goddess: Evolution of an Image* [New York: Viking, 1991] 304); or to Phoebe (l. 14), the Moon, a goddess also called Artemis and Selene; or, by implication, even to Clotho, in Greek and Roman mythology the Fate who spins the thread of life that Lachesis measures and that Atropos cuts. *The Man in the Moon*

He tugs at the boulder; samples its trace; / Manipulates an asteroid in space: In NASA's developing Asteroid Redirect Mission (ARM), astronauts will test the advanced Primary Life Support System (PLSS) even as they "collect asteroid samples during the crewed portion" of the operation. See Erin Mahoney, ed., "How Will NASA's Asteroid Redirect Mission Help Humans Reach Mars?" *NASA Asteroid Redirect Mission* 27 June 2014: 2 <www.nasa.gov>. *The Heavenly Journey of the Shaman*

heuristic: in Computer Science, a step-by-step, rule-of-thumb technique that proceeds along empirical lines and that enables the pupil (or the machine) to discover or to learn, as in this poem, a shortcut to a seemingly insoluble problem. *The Jesus of Psychoanalysis*

hierophant: either "a priest of a mystery cult," as in ancient Greece ("Hierophant" [n.], def. 1), or "a person confidently expounding, explaining, or promoting something mysterious or obscure as though appointed to do so" (def. 2). *The Woman in the Moon*

his astronaut's beat: the cyborg's "habitual path or round of duty" ("Beat" [n.], def. 4a). *Christ on Einstein's Tram*

His brazen serpent: the bronze *serpent* that Moses erected at Yahweh's command as a prefiguration of the salvific Christ. See Num. 21.4-9. *Here Be Dragons*

His fiber strewn, a microscopic thread, / Elaborate textile: In *The Body in Question* (New York: Vintage-Random, 1982), Jonathan Miller reminds us that, by the end of the eighteenth century, "biologists were confident that they had found a fundamental unit common to all the tissues of the body—a simple, irreducible element which could be put together in various ways to produce all the known textures. This unit was the fibre, a microscopic thread which could be woven into loose meshes or dense, impermeable sheets, tightly bound into tendons or loosely bundled to form muscles. By 1800 the body was seen as an elaborate textile, a garment of hemps, worsted and linens—the fact that the term 'tissue' was introduced at that time indicates the persuasiveness of the metaphor." Later, with the discovery of the cell, "biologists identified in one and the same entity the site of the [genetic] instructions and the agent [double-stranded DNA] which executed them" (266). *Spacetime's Wight*

His heart Hermetic: the heavenly *heart* of "the deathless Original Man, to whom the mortal man can be approximated by means of the alchemical opus" (*Alchemical Studies* 166). In *Hermetic* philosophy, the *heart* is "the seat of the soul" (Jung, *Psychology and Alchemy* 343n62). See also the note on *Hermetic* given above. *Schrödinger's Cat*

His Mother the Moon, His Father the Sun: an excerpt from the exordium in the "Tabula Smaragdina," where the legendary first alchemist and emblematic magus Hermes Trismegistus describes "the 'sun-moon' child who is laid in the cradle of the four elements, attains full power through them and the earth, rises to heaven and receives the power of the upper world, and then returns to earth, accomplishing, it seems, a triumph of wholeness" (Jung, *Mysterium Coniunctionis* 219). The original article from Hermes' text reads as follows: "Its father is the sun, its mother the moon; the wind hath carried it in his belly; its nurse is the earth." However, in this poem, equally pertinent is the description of the second Adam in Jung, *Aion* 221n157: "'Jesus is a synthesis and a growth, and the resultant form is one which tells of a hundred forces which went to its making. But the interesting thing is that the process did not end with the closing of the canon. Jesus is still in the making.'" The original source is R. Roberts, "Jesus or Christ? — A Reply," *The Quest* 2 (London, 1911) 124. *Containment and the Cosmic Edge*

His sapphirine power: The sapphire was one of the precious stones that "adorned" the Garden of Eden (Ezek. 28.13). Thus, according to the philosophical alchemists, the "sapphirine material" contained "that liquid in which there is no harmful matter" (Jung, *Alchemical Studies* 187n22). See also Jung's pertinent remark in *Psychology and Alchemy* 80, including fig. 30: "the golden flower of alchemy [. . .] can sometimes be a blue flower: 'The sapphire blue flower of the hermaphrodite.'" *Christ on Einstein's Tram*

His soul like an eye—the loop that you splice—: i.e., "a splice made by turning back the end of a rope and interlacing its strands into the body of the rope so as to form an end loop, or eye" ("Eye Splice," def.). The simile underscores Jakob Böhme's belief that "The soul is 'a fiery Eye'" (Jung, *The Archetypes and the Collective Unconscious* 336). *The Man in the Moon*

His tabernacled Son: As Andrew Murray reminds us in *The Spirit of Christ*, "Each of us must learn to know that there is a Holiest of All in that temple which we are" (210). In other words, because "The Spirit united itself with what would otherwise be dead matter" (166), Christ indwells or *tabernacles* His believer-priests. *Circumambient*

History's pelf: The speaker compares the Risen Savior—"The foetus in the room" (l. 8)—to treasure, wealth, or riches, the positive synonyms of *pelf*. *Trapeze*

His unit tethered: the NASA astronaut, here attached to an umbilical line or safety tether. *Scion*

His wall of jasper: Cf. Rev. 21.18, where John describes the holy city of Jerusalem at endtime: "The wall was built of jasper, while the [eternal] city itself was of pure gold, bright as clear glass." In the Bible, *jasper* is "a precious stone, probably an opaque green quartz" ("Jasper" [n.], def. 2). *Spacetime's Wight*

hoist; alight / That we may hitch a ride, without a bight, / Upon a foot restraint: a nod to the portable foot restraints that were "a standard crew aid on shuttle and International Space Station missions" and that NASA astronauts used as "a stable platform to stand on wherever they needed to work outside the spacecraft." Thus, whenever an astronaut serviced the Hubble Space Telescope, he placed mounting brackets for the foot restraints, strategically, around the shuttle payload bay and on the telescope to give him access to various worksites. "The spacewalker inserted the adjustable shaft into a bracket and then secured both booted feet under the toe bridges and into the heel clips." See "Foot Restraint, EVA, Portable, Hubble Space Telescope," Smithsonian *National Air and Space Museum* 3 <https://airandspace.si.edu>. Accessed 10 Mar. 2022. Incidentally, here, the playful *bight* is "a loop or slack part in a rope" ("Loop" [n.], def. 2). *The Moon in Transition Raised to the Sun*

holon: a whole embedded in larger wholes; hence, an entity—whether an atom or a universe—that is both a whole and a part. Arthur Koestler coined the term in *The Ghost in the Machine* (1967; New York: Arkana-Penguin, 1990) 48. *Bootstrap; Rebis*

Homunculus: "a little man; dwarf; manikin" ("Homunculus" [n.], def.). See also Jung, *The Archetypes and the Collective Unconscious* 293: "at the end of the *opus alchymicum,* the homunculus emerges, that is, the Anthropos, the spiritual, inner and complete man, who in Chinese alchemy is called the *chen-yen* (literally, 'perfect man')." Jung illustrates the concept vividly in *Psychology and Alchemy* 301, fig. 153, where the "artist" lifts "the homunculus, the 'son of the philosophers,' out of the Hermetic vessel." *The Water That Does Not Make the Hands Wet*

Hosea's claim: i.e., that the Church is the bride of Christ, the all-inclusive, firstborn Son of God. See Hos. 2.20: "'I will betroth you to myself to have and to hold, and you shall know the Lord.'" However, "the greatest turning to God is to take place in the future" (J. Vernon McGee, *Thru the Bible with J. Vernon McGee, Volume III: Proverbs through Malachi* [Nashville: Nelson, 1982] 656). *Courtship*

Hubble: i.e., the *Hubble* Space Telescope, named after Edwin Powell *Hubble* (1889-1953), an American astronomer who recognized, along with other astronomers, that the universe is expanding. Launched on the Space Shuttle *Discovery* on 24 April 1990, *Hubble,* the observatory, "is the first major optical telescope to be placed in space, the ultimate mountaintop. [. . .] Scientists have used Hubble to observe the most distant stars and galaxies as well as the planets in our solar system." See Rob Garner, "About the Hubble Space Telescope," *NASA* 2 <www.nasa.gov>. Last updated on 12 December 2017. [NB: NASA launched the James Webb Space Telescope, its successor to the *Hubble,* on 25 December 2021.] *Chain-Linked*

Hub in the tin, / The cortex shambles; modifies its spin; / While Robonaut bobbles, bootstraps the din: See Harth, *Windows on the Mind,* where the author examines "patterns of neural activity" in the human brain; argues the thesis "that thoughts are just rumblings in the cortex but often involve the nervous system at all levels"; and even illustrates the concept of "delayed consciousness" (98-99). "Consciousness, it turns out, is a slow phenomenon." In fact, "about half a second elapses before we can become conscious of an event [that] our senses have picked up" (100). Thus, Harth maintains that "the sensory [nerve] pathways are not unidirectional" but form "a *hub* of many intersecting loops"; as a result, "the stimulating, conjecturing, confabulating [cerebral] cortex can influence the stream of incoming information," thereby "producing new and modified inputs for itself." However, although "The seeds of thought may spring up anywhere in the nervous system," Harth adds that "a fully developed thought requires more than the neocortex. Thinking is a *bootstrap* mechanism." It needs a set of instructions. Indeed, "It may be as absurd to expect thought from a brain without an attached body as it would be to expect consciousness from a body without a brain" (102). *Bootstrap*

hyaline: resembling glass, like the Christian Savior and His equally transparent coheirs at End-time. *Light of the Eye*

hyperspace: "higher-dimensional space"—according to superstring theory, "the three dimensions of space (length, width, and breadth) and one of time [. . .] extended by six more spatial dimensions" (Kaku, *Hyperspace* vii-viii). *Bootstrap; The Path of Least Action; Rite*

hyphenate furled: either the speaker, the still-gestating mystic traveler "curled or rolled up" ("Furl" [vi.], def.) in the fabric of spacetime, or alchemy's spagyric foetus, or "the Son of Man whose home is in heaven" (John 3.13). Here, of course, the *hyphenate* is a person of mixed origin or identity. See the notes on *spagyric* and *The spagyric foetus spun in his womb* given below. *Bootstrap*

I approach His room: i.e., the Cenacle, "the *room* in which Jesus and [H]is disciples ate the Last Supper" ("Cenacle" [n.], def.). *The Round Dance of the Stars*

I balance my body; [. . .] with suede preserve / More than the walker: the braid that I serve: The speaker develops a metaphysical conceit—an extended metaphor—that yokes together tightrope walking and the parallel goal of the individuation process, the equally slippery "synthesis of the self" (Jung, *The Archetypes and the Collective Unconscious* 164). See also John Calhoun, "Philippe Petit: The True Story Behind the Daredevil's World Trade Center Walk," *Biography* 29 Sept. 2015 <www.biography.com>. Petit, the high-wire acrobat, took his walk between the newly-erected Twin Towers, in New York City, on 7 August 1974. *Trapeze*

I bridge all Spacetime to the Paschal Lamb; / [. . .] *Become what I will and am what I am:* The God-man—the "hierophant" of line 9—"coalesces with Christ" and Christ with "the inner ['complete'] man, the self." His "illuminated" followers "say therefore: 'I become what I will, and I am what I am'" (Jung, *Aion* 200-01). *Extract of the Macrocosm*

I glimpse a shape like a Catherine-wheel: Cf. the "spinning pinwheel" hypothesis in Patrick Moore, *Travellers in Space and Time* (New York: Doubleday, 1984) 9: "assume that the [imaginary] Andromedan astronomer is able to use a telescope as powerful as anything we have yet built on Earth. Now he will see real detail; the shape of the system [that contains our own sun] will be revealed as a rather loose spiral, like a Catherine-wheel, with dark 'lanes' here and there which he will know to be made up of dusty material, not lit up by any suitable star" (9). *Scout*

I have lived with You; eaten from Your plate / Cislunar manna; mingled like a mate: The speaker, an absolved and reconciled Christian, understands that, through the Sacrifice of the Mass, he "becomes once again supernaturally pleasing to God and capable of union with Him" (Thomas Merton, *The Living Bread* [1956; New York: Dell, 1959] 62). *The Chariot of Aristotle's Wheels*

I lift my hand to my mouth and then track: In *Being Born* (New York: Grosset, 1986), a book about "what a child could see, hear, and feel and do deep inside the mother's body, and about the baby's experience of birth" (5), Sheila Kitzinger suggests that "Your fingers were the first things you played with. They moved like the fronds of a sea anemone in a rock pool. Then one day your fingers found your mouth and brushed your lips. You liked the feeling and you began to suck your hand. Gradually you learned to bring your hand to your mouth. And then, one day, you popped your thumb in and sucked it for the very first time" (42-43). Throughout *Being Born,* in order "to retrace that adventure of the nine months of prenatal life" (5), Kitzinger supplements her observant text with Lennart Nilsson's virtuosic photographs. *The Heavenly Journey of the Shaman*

I look down first and then farther away; / Examine ancient light; impeach its ray: The speaker confronts spacetime and the indeterminacy of human perception. Stuart Clark reflects upon this conundrum in *The Unknown Universe: A New Exploration of Time, Space, and Cosmology* (New York: Pegasus, 2016) 5: "As an archeologist digs down through older and older layers of the Earth to see the pattern of evolution, so astronomers look further and further away. The further they set their gaze, the longer it has taken light to cross that distance," and "the older the celestial objects [that] they see." Thus, "If something were 1 light year away, its light would have taken a year to reach us," and "we would be seeing it as it appeared one year ago, when it emitted the light." However, "There would be no way to know what it looks like now." *Channeling Hipparchus*

An *imago mundi:* here, the Ouroboros, both mercurial serpent and "tail-eater" (Jung, *Psychology and Alchemy* 292-93)—in "the circulatory *opus,*" an image of the world "imprinted [as an archetype] in the heart of matter" and "reflected in the unconscious" (386). *Mastermind*

Impalpable its point: in astrophysics, the big-bang singularity, the imperceptible *point* of infinite compression from which the entire cosmos "erupted" (Greene, *The Elegant Universe* 83). In other words, however incomprehensible the idea may seem, at the first space-time moment, the matter of the universe was "squeezed into a single point" (Davies, *The Mind of God* 49) and then ballooned in size after the big bang in a period called inflation.

Of course, here, the speaker is aware of an alternate scenario called "the 'big bounce' model, in which our universe rose from the ashes of an earlier cosmos that ended in a 'big crunch,' a process set to repeat" when the world comes to an end, because, theoretically, "The universe can shrink to zero and reappear, and the light is never wiser." See Lisa Grossman, "Our universe could be reborn as a bouncing baby cosmos," *New Scientist* 11 July 2016: 2-3 <www.newscientist.com>. *Splitting the Earth with a Straight Foot*

Implicates the spheroid: a cosmic pun. The speaker refers to the flattened shape of the earth, an oblate *spheroid,* "a body that is almost but not quite a sphere" ("Spheroid" [n.], def.), even as he broaches another subject, the implicate order, a worldview proposed by David Bohm (1917-1994), a renowned theoretical scientist. In this model of reality—as in a hologram—any element contains, enfolded within itself, the totality of the universe. In fact, here, the word *implicate* also suggests "a connection with a crime [or a] fault," the fatal first sin of Adam and Eve ("Implicate" [vt.], def. 1a). *Storyboard*

In a patch of desert I test my will, / Hook up a screen that with data I fill: a simulated visit to the Martian terrain. See Shannon Stirone, "A Drill to Tunnel Miles Below the Surface of Mars," *Popular Science* 2 Dec. 2015: 1-4 <www.popsci.com>: "It's noon in Ocotillo Wells, California. A vast and empty patch of desert between San Diego and the Salton Sea, this part of California might as well be Mars. After just a few minutes, everything is covered with a fine white dust, soft to the touch, like a powdered sugar. Kris Zacny, the vice president and director of Honeybee Robotics, grabs his hardhat and vest out of his car and walks over to a U-Haul that is serving as mission control. Today, Zacny and his team will begin testing the Planetary Deep Drill, designed to penetrate miles under the surface of places like Mars and Europa to search for one thing: evidence of life. [. . .] the Planetary Deep Drill contains a microscope, cameras, and LED and UV lights. The UV light will help [to] identify microbes and minerals that fluoresce [in the off-Earth site]." However, the drill "is not yet scheduled to launch to another planet, and couldn't do so for another decade." *Drilling on Mars*

In baptismal waters that coheirs bless, / Or pail or *opus,* afloat we caress: See Jung, *Psychology and Alchemy* 380-81: "In the Manichaean system the savior constructs a cosmic wheel with twelve buckets—the zodiac—for the raising of souls. This wheel has a significant connection with the *rota* [or circulatory *opus*] of alchemy, which serves the same purpose of sublimation," and with the sun-god or [sun]-hero who submits to arduous labours and to the passion of self-cremation, like Herakles [and Christ], or to captivity and dismemberment at the hands of the evil principle, like Osiris." Equally pertinent is "the fiery chariot in which Elijah ascended to heaven" [2 Kings 2.11]. See also Kitzinger and Nilsson, *Being Born,* where the warm foetus swam fishlike "in a bubble of water" (30). *The Woman in the Moon*

In Him the doors of the solstices sown: The speaker refers to John 10.7: "I [Jesus Christ] am the door" and to 1 John 1.5: "God is Light, and in him there is no darkness at all." See also *Stars, Planets, and Galaxies* 14, where Engelbrektson explains that "[t]he origin of the word solstice means '(the) sun (has) stood still'" and that, in "its path across the sky," the disseminated sun "reaches the [summer and winter] solstices on June 21 and December 21 in the solar calendar employed in many countries throughout the world." *Gateway*

in many vases / His afterbirth yet preserved: This statement is merely suppositional, since, according to Jewish purity laws, the midwives "would have taken the placenta [. . .] and buried it" outside the city of Bethlehem, the birthplace of Christ (Elizabeth Fletcher, "Jesus is born in Bethlehem," *Jesus: stories, gospel study questions, text 5* <www.womeninthebible.net/Elizabeth_bible_text.htm>). Accessed 23 Feb. 2020. *The Jesus of Psychoanalysis*

In rock at first, in forebrow, or in mist: a triad of testaments to the "almost limitless range of the [archetypal] self" (Jung, *Psychology and Alchemy* 19). Thus, Mithras, the Persian sun-god, emerged from a *rock;* Athena, the Greek warrior-goddess, sprang from the forehead of Zeus; and Aphrodite, the Greek love-goddess, rose from either sea-spume or pillars of *mist*. *Extract from the Macrocosm*

Instinct: a desideratum of the transcendental self. See Jung, *Aion* 247-48n79: "With the loss of symbolic ideas the bridge to the unconscious has broken down. Instinct no longer affords protection against unsound ideas and empty slogans. Rationality without tradition and without a basis in instinct is proof against no absurdity." *Extract of the Macrocosm*

Intermezzo of winds: See *Symbols of Trans*formation 316-17, where Jung explains that, in the second canto of *The Song of Hiawatha* [an epic poem by Henry Wadsworth Longfellow], through the "caressing courtship" of the West Wind, with his "fertilizing breath," and the East Wind, with her "blue eyes like [t]wo blue lakes," rebirth beckons the hero because "from 'wind and water' man shall be born anew." In effect, soul attracts spirit (316n18). *Splitting the Earth with a Straight Foot*

intertwined its strands, / [. . .] balsam in the bands: In *Alchemical Studies,* Jung remarks that Paracelsus, the 16th-century philosophical alchemist, "attributes incorruptibility to a special virtue or agent named 'balsam.' This was something like a natural elixir, by means of which the body was kept alive or, if dead, incorruptible." In other words, "The balsam is the life principle [. . .]" (134-35). Thus, "Like the [spectrum of the white] sun in the heavens, the balsam in the heart is a fiery, radiant centre" (152). See also the note on *It drips from the sun and produces gold* given below. *Ephesian Symbols*

In the cloud a foetus: i.e., the spagyric *foetus*. The word *spagyric* refers to an alchemical process that both separates and combines (Jung, *Mysterium Coniunctionis* 481n91). Thus, the spagyric *foetus* ascends into Heaven that it may become a spirit from a body and then descends to earth that it may become a body again. Cf. John 3.13: "No one ever went up into heaven except the one who came down from heaven, the Son of Man whose home is in heaven." *Light of the Eye*

in the Moon he sits: Jung notes that "in Plutarch [c. AD 46-120] Hermes [god of revelation and guide of souls] sits in the moon and goes round with it (just as Heracles does in the sun)." In effect, the *Moon* is the white "receptacle of souls" (*Mysterium Coniunctionis* 140). *Fabricator*

in the spheroid that He spun: i.e., whether physically or psychologically, in the *oblate* spheroid, here "the slightly flattened" shape of either the Earth, the Moon, or the Sun. See Duncan Steel, *Eclipse: The Celestial Phenomenon That Changed the Course of History* (Washington, DC: Joseph Henry, 2001) 51. *Claim*

In the vas all gold, the glass that anneals: In *Alchemical Studies* 197-98, Jung reminds us that the Hermetic vessel "had to be made of glass, since it was meant to represent the cosmos in which the earth was created." Since transparent glass "is something like solidified water or air, both of which are synonyms for spirit," the alchemical retort "is therefore equivalent to the *anima mundi* [the soul of the world], which according to an old alchemical conception surrounds the cosmos." Jung adds that, in the arcane teaching of alchemy, the soul has also appeared as "a spherical glass vessel" and that the philosophers' stone was "often equated with the gold glass (*aureum vitreum*) of the heavenly Jerusalem (Rev. 21.21)." Of course, here the term *anneals* has a double-edged meaning—not only "to heat [glass or metals] and then cool slowly to prevent brittleness," but also "to strengthen and temper the mind [and] will" ("Anneal" [vt.], defs. 2, 3). *The Chariot of Aristotle's Wheels*

In the vas of the moon all men die twice: In *The Penguin Dictionary of Symbols,* Chevalier and Gheerbrant note that "'The moon, as Plutarch remarked, is where good men go after they die. There they lead a life which may not be godlike, but is yet free from care until they die for a second time. All men must die twice.' Thus the Moon is the abode of individuals between the time when they leave their bodies and the second death which is the prologue to their rebirth" (675). [The quoted passage is from Gérard van Rijnberk, *Le tarot: histoire, iconographie, ésotérisme* (Lyon, 1947: 252).] Obviously, in this poem, in view of the NASA astronaut's extraterrestrial journey, Plutarch's allusion to rebirth is highly pertinent. However, in the speaker's "numinous" dream of the wandering microcosm embodied by the mortal man, although the astronaut "points to the Messiah" (ll. 2, 17), and although, like Christ, he is destined to be "Reborn" (l. 3), his "higher man"—the "Astral symbolon" of line 20—is not yet a "perfect" man and is "not [yet] clearly formed" (Jung, *Aion* 213-14). *The Man in the Moon*

Inwards of the head: See Jung, *Mysterium Coniunctionis* 423: "Since sun and gold are equivalent concepts in alchemy, the *solificatio* means that the 'inwards of the head' [. . .] are transformed into light [. . .]." Jung adds that, "as the head is illuminated, so the heart burns in love." Not surprisingly, then, "The brain is of interest to the alchemists because it was the seat of the 'spirit of the supracelestial waters'" and is thus the "'abode of the divine part'" (435). In other words, the "transformation [of consciousness] takes place in the head and is a psychic process" (*Alchemical Studies* 88). *Ephesian Symbols*

I opened the hatch, stood up in my seat: In this stanza, the suited NASA astronaut exits his spacecraft through "a special door called an airlock." During the spacewalk, he uses ropelike tethers that keep him from "floating away," one end "hooked to the spacewalker" and the other end "connected to the vehicle." Not insignificantly, the astronaut wears a

SAFER, i.e., a Simplified Aid for EVA [Extra-Vehicular Activity] rescue, a self-contained, propulsive backpack system fueled by nitrogen-fed jet thrusters that enable the astronaut to "move around in space." The astronaut controls SAFER "with a small joystick." See Flint Wild, "What Is a Spacewalk?" NASA 27 July 2020: 1-3 <www.nasa.gov>. See also the note on *He opens the hatch, stands up in his seat* given above. *Circumambient*

I orbit the moon till day and night pall; / Float into my pouch: Here, the speaker is not only the human embryo forming in the womb and then, later, the curled-up foetus developing inside the amniotic sac, but also the sealed NASA astronaut orbiting the moon in his space capsule. *The Heavenly Journey of the Shaman*

iota: "the smallest Greek character, corresponding to our 'dot' (which did not exist in Greek)." See Jung, *Aion* 218n135 and also the note on *jot* given below. *The Smoke-Hole of the Tent*

I rise in the omniverse like a bead: i.e., like "a drop [of sweat]" or "a bubble in an effervescing liquid" ("Bead" [n.], defs. 5, 6). See also the note on "sweat" given below. *Extract of the Macrocosm*

I scrape its surface with my fingernail: In line 22, the brittle "gypsum [rock] in a pail" is "a close analog to ice that has been evaporated and re-condensed on planetary surfaces for millions of years." Nevertheless, although you "might be able to scrape the surface with your fingernail, drilling kilometers down requires a tool strong enough to break through the [layered] ice and rock" (Stirone, "A Drill to Tunnel Miles Below the Surface of Mars" 6). *Drilling on Mars*

I spiral in her womb, and then I stall: In *Being Born,* Sheila Kitzinger describes and Lennart Nilsson photographs "the nine-month journey from conception to birth." Thus, addressing the developing foetus, Kitzinger writes that, after seven months, "When you felt the thick, springy uterus pressing against your foot, you pressed your foot down and then lifted it. You took your first step. The stepping movements you made helped you turn upside down in the uterus, ready to be born. They helped you press your way out of the uterus when it was time to be born" (52-53). *A Methane Snow*

I still invite the kite: i.e., the black *kite*—here, a substitute for the raven, the latter bird a symbol of "the *nigredo* or blackness" in the crucial initial stage of the alchemical [or psychic] transformation process (Jung, *Psychology and Alchemy* 230, fig. 115). *Rite*

I switch on a bulb in a darkened room, / The delay so slight before light can loom / On an opposite wall, in space or womb / I contemplate Ge's Andromedan gloom: Cf. Moore, *Travellers in Space and Time* 9: "Light moves faster than anything else in the universe, but it does not travel instantaneously. Switch on a torch in a darkened room, and there will be a definite interval before the beam reaches the opposite wall, though the delay is so slight that it could certainly not be measured. Light takes one and a quarter seconds to reach us from the Moon, which is much closer to us than any other natural body in the sky. This is trifling; but with the Andromeda Spiral, the situation is different, and our present-day view of it is very out of date, because the light we are just [now] receiving from it started on its journey towards us over 2,000,000 years ago, well before the beginning of the last Ice Age." See also *Stars, Planets, and Galaxies,* where Engelbrektson reminds us that, "In the northern hemisphere, a huge spiral of a billion stars called the *Andromeda Galaxy* appears on the threshold of vision in the constellation of Andromeda, between Pisces and Cassiopeia" (23). *Scout*

I take a risk— / Joined with Atlas, I commandeer each disk: In these lines, the *risk*-taking speaker identifies with *Atlas,* the heroic Titan who—having been defeated in the war against the Olympians and condemned by Zeus—"bore the world on his shoulders" as his eternal punishment (Hamilton, *Mythology* 25). *Channeling Hipparchus*

It drips from the sun and produces gold: In alchemy, the "active sun-substance," despite its "Typhonian" or satanic nature, "also has favourable effects." Thus, as "the so-called 'balsam' it drips from the sun and produces lemons, oranges, wine, and, in the mineral kingdom, gold" (Jung, *Mysterium Coniunctionis* 93). Presumably, "Just as the physical sun lightens and warms the universe, so, in the human body, there is in the heart a sunlike arcanum from which life and warmth stream forth" (94). *The Water That Does Not Make the Hands Wet*

I tipped the cone; / Assembled all my souls: The NASA astronaut refers to the light *cone,* "the wall of light that separates our reality and other realities." In effect, "All light beams coming from a given point move along the light cone" (Bob Toben, "in conversation with" Jack Sarfatti and Fred Wolf, *Space-Time and Beyond: Toward an Explanation of the Unexplainable* [New York: Dutton, 1975] 28). Furthermore, light cones that tip may even allow "time-travel into another universe," or "into one's own past" (133). Of course, in this excerpt, the speaker also echoes the "primitive assertion that the [holistic] individual has a plurality of souls" (Jung, *Mysterium Coniunctionis* 358n386). *Chain-Linked*

It is done: These words permeate a scene redolent of ritual death and mythical sacrifice, like the new moon phase portrayed in the second stanza and the full moon phase in this, the third. Significantly, Mary—here, both Co-Redemptrix *and* Mother—echoes Jesus' *tetelestai,* their cost-split, for the bill marked *paid in full.* Cf. John 19.28-30: After His crucifixion, "Jesus, aware that all had now come to its appointed end, said in fulfillment of Scripture, 'I thirst.' A jar stood there full of sour wine; so they [or even only one witness] soaked a sponge with the wine, fixed it on a javelin [or on a sprig of hyssop], and held it up to his lips. Having received the wine, he said, 'It is accomplished!' He bowed his head and gave up his spirit." *The Woman in the Moon*

I tossed my stone / To the other side: See Jung, *Alchemical Studies* 101: "The connection of the lapis [the magical Hermetic stone] with immortality is attested from very early times." Thus, in a South African legend reported by the ethnologist Leo Frobenius (1873-1938), "the hero is left stranded by his pursuers on the bank of a river. He changes himself into a stone, and his pursuers throw him across to the other side. This is the motif of the *transitus:* the 'other side' is the same as eternity." *Circumambient*

I track a cloud, His soul-spark, and then, fleet [. . .], / the scion in the pleat: in the unconscious psyche, a synchronistic phenomenon; a coincidence in time of two or more causally unrelated events—here, cloud and deity—that "have the same or a similar meaning" (C. G. Jung, *Synchronicity: An Acausal Connecting Principle,* trans. R. F. C. Hull [1960; Princeton: Princeton UP, 1973] 25).   Jung suggests that, when "one or more external events [. . .] appear as meaningful parallels to the [perceiver's] momentary subjective state," there must be "some archetypal symbolism at work" (23).   In other words, the emergence in time of meaningful coincidences "cannot be explained without the hypothesis of the collective unconscious" (24), a substratum of the human brain "transcending all differences in culture and consciousness" (Jung, *Alchemical Studies* 11).   Thus, according to Jung, "Christ is an autonomous image"—an inborn symbol of rebirth—that, as an instance of *a priori* psychic orderedness, "can be directly experienced" (247). *A Methane Snow*

its animate stone: the transformational *lapis*—in effect, the *stone* that has a spirit: "the figure of light veiled in matter" (Jung, *Alchemical Studies* 247), a symbolic "parallel of Christ" (96).   See also 1 Pet. 2.5: "Come, and let yourselves be built, as living stones, into a spiritual temple; become a holy priesthood, to offer spiritual sacrifices acceptable to God through Jesus Christ." *Christ on Einstein's Tram*

Its binary choices even as staves / Or, incorporeal, those Forms in caves: Like *staves* or stanzas in a poem, the world accommodates such opposites as Heaven and Earth, Sun and Moon, Above and Below, light and darkness, Man and Woman, consciousness and unconsciousness, Spirit and Body, wave and particle, and—as in Plato's philosophy—eternal models: the soul's essential Forms ("Idea" [n.], def. 7) and material things.   See also the note on *Even as opposites rise in the stave* given above, along with the note on *those Forms in caves* given below. *Storyboard*

It spins like a marble: Seen from outer space, Earth—our home planet— "looks like a blue marble with white swirls" (Flint Wild, ed., "What Is Earth?" NASA 4 Oct. 2017: 1 <www.nasa.gov>). *Fixated on Mars*

Its point Archimedean (ar-kuh-mi-DEE-in): In *Psychology and Western Religion,* Jung insists that, as a Christian disciple, "you would not be able to understand what you suffer unless there were that Archimedean point outside, the objective standpoint of the [noumenal] self, from which the ego can be seen as a phenomenon. Without the objectification of the self the ego would remain caught in hopeless subjectivity and would only gyrate round itself" (176-77). For further insight into this Jungian thesis, see the note on *I will be united* and on *The Round Dance of the Stars* given below. Incidentally, the reference to Archimedes is pertinent: He was a 3rd-century Greek mathematician who, having hypothesized "a god's-eye view" of things, supposedly said that "with a fulcrum for the lever he could move the earth" (Bronowski, *The Ascent of Man* 74). *Scintilla's Scan*

Its wheels quaternal, like faces that furl: The chariot with four wheels is the sun, "the mercurial serpent," here identical not only with "the sun-god or [sun]–hero who submits to arduous labours and to the passion of self-cremation, like Herakles" on the night-sea journey, but also with "the [arcane] substance to be transformed" in the Hermetic vessel

(Jung, *Psychology and Alchemy* 381-82). In addition, the image recalls the "four living creatures"—the fiery Cherubim—that appear in Ezekiel 1.5, each of them with four faces and with four wings, and each "like a wheel [folded] inside a wheel" (Ezek. 1.17), moving "in whatever direction the spirit would go" (20) and—as Jung observes in his discussion of the transformation process elsewhere—"performing those cyclic evolutions which bring the mandala of the total personality, the ground-plan of the self, closer to consciousness" (Jung, *Mysterium Coniunctionis* 204). *Mastermind*

It was not a house, a cloud, or a jar— / A drop of liquid absorbed by a spar: / Residual coupling: In *Other Worlds,* Paul Davies reminds us that a "central feature of [the] Newtonian view of a real world is the existence of identifiable 'things'" to which "intrinsic attributes" can "consistently be ascribed." In daily life "we have no difficulty in accepting, for example, a football as a football—a definite entity with fixed properties (round, leathery, hollow . . .)." In other words, "It is not a house or a cloud or a star." However, in the macroscopic world, objects "are distinct [only] so long as their mutual interaction is in some sense small." Thus, "[w]hen a drop of liquid falls into the ocean it interacts strongly with the larger body of water and becomes absorbed into it, losing its identity completely." By contrast, "when objects are separated by a large distance, we think of them as being distinct: the planets of the solar system, the atoms in London and New York, etc." In fact, since "all known forces of interaction diminish rapidly with distance, [. . .] well-separated entities [appear to] behave almost independently." Still, they are "never completely independent—there is always a residual coupling between all things" (109), whether by chance or by choice (145), as even the quantum theory of the world suggests (135, 138). *Schrödinger's Cat*

I uncoiled my tether, dangled my feet, / Then floated there, exhilarated, fleet. / All life is real, Castor, when it is shown: In his blissful dream life, the astronaut—in edgeless, elastic spacetime, both "the mass and a [mere] particle in the mass"—becomes, momentarily, spirit-substance: an empirical manifestation of the still-gestating, numinous, illimitable self. Cf. Jung, *Psychology and Alchemy* 81: "Life that just happens in and for itself is not real life; it is real only when it is *known.*" Thus, Jung insists that "Psychology is concerned with the act of seeing" (13), even as, empirically, "it opens people's eyes to the real meaning of dogmas" (15) and to "the 'eternal' presence" (221) of the archetypes of the collective unconscious. Nietzsche's metaphor in *Thus Spake Zarathustra*—"'an image slumbers for me in the stone'" [to which Jung alludes (296)]—is also pertinent here. *Circumambient*

I will be united: a theme that underscores the speaker's Christological focus. Thus, in the Acts of John, "one of the most important of the apocryphal texts that have come down to us," the author describes "a mystical 'round dance' which Christ instituted before his crucifixion. He told his disciples to hold hands and form a ring, while he himself stood in the centre. As they moved around, Christ sang a song of praise" that included a key verse: "'I will be united and I will unite. Amen'" (Jung, *Psychology and Western Religion* 169-70). According to Jung, these words mean that "subjective consciousness is united with an objective centre, thus producing the unity of God and man represented by Christ." In effect, "Christ, or the self, is a 'mirror': on the one hand it reflects the subjective consciousness of the disciple, making it visible to him, and on the other hand it 'knows' Christ, that is to say it does not merely reflect the empirical man, it also shows him as a (transcendental) whole." In other words, "when you relate to your own (transcendental) centre, you initiate a process of conscious development which leads to oneness and wholeness. You no longer see yourself as an isolated point on the periphery, but as the One in the centre." In fact, "The paradoxical identity and difference of ego and self could hardly be formulated more trenchantly" (176-77). See the note on *I will be wounded* and on *The Round Dance of the Stars* given below. *Scintilla's Scan*

    I will be wounded: The speaker "refers to the wound in Christ's side" (Jung, *Psychology and Western Religion* 174) even as he highlights "the mystical 'round dance'" that, according to the Acts of John, a New Testament apocryphal text, "Christ instituted before his crucifixion" (169). Thus, "He told his disciples to hold hands and form a ring, while he himself stood in the centre" (169-70). Significantly, in the Last Supper, "there is an ingestion and assimilation of the Lord," whereas, in the round dance, a rite reminiscent of a pagan feast, "there is a circular circumambulation round the Lord as the central point." Nevertheless, Jung notes that, "Despite the outward difference of the symbols, they have a common meaning: Christ is taken into the midst of the disciples" as the supernal source of "synthesis and union" (171). *The Round Dance of the Stars*

    Jachin [yah-KEEN] and Boaz [BOH-az]: See 1 Kings 7: 14-22: "Hiram [the artisan from Tyre] came to King Solomon and executed all his works. He cast in a mould the two bronze pillars [prominent in the temple]. [. . .] When he had erected the pillar on the right side, he named it Jachin [meaning *It shall stand*]; and when he had erected the one on the left side, he named it Boaz [meaning *In strength*]." According to J. Vernon McGee, these two pillars symbolize both "the power of God in delivering [the believer-priest] from sin" and "the beauty of holiness" (*Thru the Bible with J. Vernon McGee, Volume II: Joshua—Psalms* [Nashville: Nelson, 1982] 262). *Gatekeeper*

    Jesus bucketed souls beyond the grave: See Jung, *Psychology and Alchemy* 380-81: "In the Manichaean system the savior constructs a cosmic wheel with twelve buckets—the zodiac—for the raising of souls. This wheel has a significant connection with the *rota* or *opus circulatorium* of alchemy, which serves the same purpose of sublimation." In other words, "The wheel turns into the wheel of the sun rolling round the heavens, and so becomes identical with the sun-god or [sun]-hero who submits to arduous labours and to the passion of self-cremation, like Herakles [and Christ], or to captivity and dismemberment at the hands of the evil principle, like Osiris. [Another] well-known parallel to the chariot of the sun is the fiery chariot in which Elijah ascended to heaven" (2 Kings 2.11). *The Jesus of Psychoanalysis*

    Jesus' nightgown: The speaker refers to the age-old religious belief that babies born in a caul—the filmy membrane or remains of the amniotic sac—are blessed. Technically, a caul birth happens "when a small piece of the lining breaks away and sticks around the baby's head, face, or both. Sometimes the piece is big enough to drape even the baby's shoulders and chest—like a see-through superhero hood and cape." However, "this is unlike an en caul birth," where [the] baby "is entirely encased in the sac" (Noreen Iftikhar, MD, and Carolyn Kay, MD, "Parenthood," *Healthline* 20 Dec. 2019: 2 <www.healthline.com>). See also James Hurst, "The Scarlet Ibis," a short story published in the July 1960 edition of *The Atlantic Monthly,* where a character believes that "cauls were made from Jesus's nightgown," and the note on *diadem in the ball* given above. *A Methane Snow*

jinn: in popular usage, a single supernatural being that can assume either human or animal form—here, in the service of Asclepius, in Greek mythology a benevolent physician presumptuous enough to raise a man from the dead. *Scout*

jot: See Jung, *Mysterium Coniunctionis* 44: "'The emblem of the whole man,'" says Monoïmos, an Arabian Gnostic, "'is the jot or tittle,'" i.e., not only "'the uncompounded, simple, unmixed Monad,'" but also "'the many-faced, thousand-eyed, and thousand-named jot of the iota'" that, "'flowing from on high, full and filling all things,'" contains "'everything that is in the Man, the Father of the Son of the Man.'" Jung suggests that the entire passage is both "a Gnostic paraphrase of John 1" and "a meaningful exposition of the psychological self" (44n25). *The Smoke-Hole of the Tent; The Water That Does Not Make the Hands Wet*

kenosis: in alchemy, a lunisolar symbol. Thus, "the 'waxing and waning' of the [lunar] bride [the Church] is based on the *kenosis"*—i.e., the emptying—"of the [solar] bridegroom [Christ], in accordance with the words of St. Ambrose" in his *Hexameron:* "'He emptied her that he might fill her, as he also emptied himself that he might fill all things. He emptied himself that he might come down to us. He came down to us that he might rise again for all'" (Jung, *Mysterium Coniunctionis* 35). See the note on *Light twines the moon* given below. *The Man in the Moon; Mastermind*

Kepler's rite: The speaker refers to the "psychic premises" of Johannes Kepler, the seventeenth-century astronomer, and to his implicit belief that the universal archetypes are "inalienable components of the empirical world-picture" (Jung, *Alchemical Studies* 289) and that cosmogonic mythology is "the quintessence of inner experience" (Jung, *Aion* 174). Thus, in this line, the NASA astronaut, beam-powered to the inner solar system (specifically, to Mars), means to imply that "'the soul in man [and in woman] is rooted in the aether'" (*Alchemical Studies* 312n11). *Drilling on Mars*

the King lies slain: In *Psychology and Alchemy,* Jung explains that "the sick king who was nevertheless born perfect is the man who suffers from spiritual sterility" (412). In effect, the king "represents the domineering conscious mind which, in the course of coming to terms with the unconscious, is swallowed up by it" (417). *Psalter*

knoll: Golgotha, the "small hill on the side of a busy road" where Christ was crucified (John Wijingaards, *Handbook to the Gospels: A Guide to the Gospel Writings and to the Life and Times of Jesus* (Michigan: Servant Books, 1979) 240. See the note on *omphalos* given below. *Evangelist*

Kobolds: here, gnomes that live "in mines and other underground places" ("Kobold" [n.], def. 2). *The Cusp of Skill; Light of the Eye*

lacunae: missing portions in a manuscript or a text. *Gateway*

lanceolate spill, / Acheulian [uh-SHOO-lee-un] tools on the cusp of skill: According to Cassandra M. Turcotte, the *Acheulian* is a technological tradition "tied to Homo erectus" and even to early homo sapiens and "characterized by an increasingly long history in the human cultural record across unprecedented geographical spans." In fact, "early occurrences of the Acheulian include the appearance of [knapped] handaxes and [biface] cleavers" ("Stone Tools," *Bradshaw Foundation* 10 Dec. 20211: 3: <www.bradshawfoundation.com>) and weapons or tools "narrow or tapering like the head of a lance" ("Lanceolate" [adj.], def.). *The Cusp of Skill*

A lance that glints: After the death of Jesus, "one of the soldiers stabbed his side with a lance, and at once there was a flow of blood [for atonement] and water [for purification]" (John 19.34). According to Professor Cahleen Shrier, both pericardial effusion and pleural effusion (the build-up of fluid around the heart and around the lungs) were among the chief causes that led to the physical death of Christ. See "The Science of the Crucifixion," *Azusa Pacific University,* March 2002: 7-8 <www.apu.edu>. *Spacetime's Wight*

the *lapis*: in alchemy, the philosophers' stone taken as a symbol of the unified self, i.e., "of the inner Christ, of God in man" (Jung, *Alchemical Studies* 96). *The Cusp of Skill*

light of the eye: Cf. Zajonc, *Catching the Light* 341: "Light, ever active, created the eye. It sculpted an organ suited to itself, like the streaming water shaping the stones over and through which it flows. Had light not 'seen' man, we should never have seen the light." *Light of the Eye*

Light twines the Moon: In *Mysterium Coniunctionis* 35-36n104, Jung, quoting Professor Hugo Rahner [1900-68], refers to "the parallel *kenosis* [emptying] of Ecclesia—Luna," a key idea of the Christian theologians. Thus, "The closer Luna approaches to the sun, the more she is darkened until, at the conjunction of the new moon, all her light is 'emptied' into Christ, the sun. [. . .] The remarkable paradox of Luna, that she is darkest when nearest the sun, is a symbol of Christian asceticism: 'The more the inward man draws nigh to the sun, the more is the outward man destroyed, but the inward man is renewed from day to day' [a variation of 2 Cor. 4.16]. That is, the Christian dies like Luna and his life is 'hid with Christ in God' [Col. 3.3]. All this Augustine says in *Epistola* 55, v, 8. Afterwards he applies it to the Church and her destiny (*Epistola* 55, vi, 10)," for "she will vanish into Christ, the sun, at the end of time [. . .]." See the note on *kenosis* given above. *Mastermind*

Like Abraham's cube: The speaker alludes to the Kaaba (KAH-buh), both a cube-shaped sanctuary and the holiest shrine in Islam. In fact, the Kaaba "is considered by Muslims to be the house of God; it rests within the Grand Mosque of Mecca" and "can be traced far back to the time of Abraham [Ibrahim]," who, along with his son Ishmael [Ismail], "is believed to have built the Kaaba on a site originally founded by Adam and Eve" (Tom O'Connor, "What Is the Kaaba? A Brief History of the Holiest Site Ahead of Hajj 2017," *Newsweek* 8 August 2017 <www.newsweek.com>). *A Methane Snow*

Like a bubble that shimmers in its pan: Cf. Kitzinger and Nilsson, *Being Born* 30, where the embryonic "ball of cells grew and grew till it looked like a shimmering, silvery blackberry" (15) and where, weeks later, the warm foetus swam fishlike "in a bubble of water." *Rebis*

Like Adam Kadmon: Here the speaker enshrines the cosmogonic mediator between Heaven and Earth, not "the 'old Adam,'" but Adam the Primordial Man, the archetype within us"—i.e., the androgynous second Adam, "the still older Adam [Kadmon] before the Fall [. . .]" (Jung, *Mysterium Coniunctionis* 452-53), both "the Original Man of Jewish gnosis" and "the product of the conjunction of sun and moon" (50-51). See the note on *Wash me, and I shall be whiter than snow* given below. *The Smoke-Hole of the Tent*

Like alphabet rings: Composed of millions of icy particles, Saturn's revolving *rings* "are named alphabetically in the order of discovery. Thus the main rings are, [. . .] farthest from the planet to closer, A, B, and C. A gap 2,920 miles wide (4,700 kilometers), known as the Cassini Division, separates the A and B rings. Other, fainter rings have been discovered as telescope technology has improved. Voyager 1 detected the innermost D ring in 1980. The F ring lies just outside of the A ring," while the G and E *rings* "lie even farther out." See Nola Taylor Redd, "Saturn's Rings: Composition, Characteristics & Creation," *Space.com* 8 Nov. 2017: 2-3 <www.space.com>. *Rite*

like a point: According to Johann Christoph Steeb, a Renaissance alchemist, "The point is most akin to the nature of light, and light is a *simulacrum Dei*" (Jung, *Alchemical Studies* 151)—i.e., a trace or a semblance or an image of God. See also *Mysterium Coniunctionis* 45, where Jung quotes another alchemist, John Dee, Steeb's contemporary: "'Things and beings have their first origin in the point and the monad.'" *Containment and the Cosmic Edge*

Like a shard through fingers sprung from its zone: either the host of shards, a symbol of "plurality and death," that, in the *Kabbala Denudata,* "[i]n consequence of the Fall [. . .] irrupted" into Adam Belial's body (Jung, *The Archetypes and the Collective Unconscious* 328n116) or, simply enough, anorthosite, a fragment of moon rock collected by Apollo 15 astronauts. *Scion*

like gum with gum: In alchemy, "the 'red' gum is the 'resin of the wise'—a synonym for the transforming substance, the glue of the world that is the medium between mind and body and the union of both." Significantly, red gum, or the viscous gold, "is duplex, i.e., masculine and feminine." So "the union of the two is a kind of self-fertilization," a characteristic underscored in a famous treatise of Maria Prophetissa, "from which comes the saying, often repeated later: 'Marry gum with gum in true marriage.'" Here, "it can be easily seen who the philosophical man is: he is the androgynous [and bisexual] original man or Anthropos of Gnosticism [. . .], whose parallel in India is *purusha.* Of him the Brihadaranyaka Upanishad says: 'He was as large as a man and woman embracing. He divided his self [Atman] in two and thence arose husband and wife. He united himself with her and men were born [. . .]" (Jung, *Psychology and Alchemy* 161-62). *Cat's Eye; Storyboard*

Like heron and kite: a pair of opposites that constitutes "the phenomenology of the paradoxical *self:* man [and woman's] totality" (Jung, *Mysterium Coniunctionis* 6). With this phrase, the speaker also conflates two stages of the alchemical process of transformation—specifically, the *nigredo* or blackness, the initial state, and the subsequent "silver or moon condition," the *albedo* or whitening. Here, of course, the *kite* or hawk is a substitute for the raven, a recurrent "*nigredo* symbol" (Jung, *Psychology and Alchemy* 230, fig. 115). Incidentally, birds with feathers that exhibit iridescence include the Tricolored Heron and the Swallow-tailed Kite. However, to grasp the full import of the concluding lines in this poem, see John 9.5: "'While I am in the world I am the light of the world,'" along with the note on *Minerals fluoresce in the presence of light* given below. *The Round Dance of the Stars*

Like soul from such blood as flows in the vein: The speaker refers to the stone that has a spirit: "the figure of light veiled in matter" (Jung, *Alchemical Studies* 247), a symbolic "parallel of Christ" (96). Not impertinently, the 16th-century Belgian alchemist Gerard Dorn suggests that "'In the blood of this stone is hidden its soul'" (qtd. in *Alchemical Studies* 291)—the *lapis* being, in the context of this poem, an analogue synonymous with the quintessence, the bridegroom, the giant of twofold substance (292nn3-5), "the mysterious filius [. . .] concocted artificially in a retort" (Jung, *Mysterium Coniunctionis* 318), and, not least of all, the universal Savior at endtime. *Evangelist*

Like the heat in the mind: Cf. *Philosophia reformata* (1622), where the Rosicrucian alchemist Johann Daniel Mylius says: "'In the shadow of the sun is the heat of the moon'" (Jung, *Mysterium Coniunctionis* 97n38), because, as Jung observes, "This view is true of all alchemical qualities, and each thing bears in itself its opposite" (98). Not surprisingly, then, in basic Hermetic discourse, the paternal sun is both "'hidden in,'" and "'extracted from,'" the maternal moon (98n42). *The Water That Does Not Make the Hands Wet*

Like the redness of the Egyptian Set: See Jung, *Mysterium Coniunctionis* 92-94: "Redness, heat, and dryness are the classical qualities of the Egyptian Set [in Greek myth, identified with Typhon], the evil principal which, like the alchemical sulphur, is closely connected with the devil." Apparently, according to the alchemists, *redness* is the "Typhonian aspect" of the ambivalent Sol, the gold that is also both the astral balsam, an "active sun-substance," and "the celestial body." *The Water That Does Not Make the Hands Wet*

Like the Seraphim: Here, the speaker—the "Quicksilver scion" of line 21—evokes the alchemical notion that "Fire with its hot and dry qualities is the most volatile element," with an energy component that "seeks to ascend," even as the radiant Seraphim in Ezekiel 1.21 moved like wheels that "rose from the ground." See Dennis William Hauck, "Working with the Elements," *The Four Elements* 2 <www.azothalchemy.org/elements.htm>. Accessed on 18 Jan. 2020. *The Round Dance of the Stars*

Like us he is not alone in the night: In "When Galaxies Collide," Sharon Begley reasons that, according to images captured by the Hubble Space Telescope, "it is a rare star that does not eventually have planets. Which makes the odds that we are not alone in the universe even shorter" (*Newsweek* 2 Nov. 1997: 3 <www.newsweek.com/when-galaxies-collide>). *Courtship*

liminal: "of or at the limen, or threshold," i.e., "at a point where one perception or condition blends or crosses over into another" ("Liminal" [adj.], defs. 1, 2). See also the matching note on *a starker rite / Than the node at new moon* given below. *Spacetime's Wight*

list: an archaic word: "to wish; like; choose" ("List"[2] [vi.], def.). *Scion*

Living stones exude a heavenly sweat: In alchemy, the mysterious *lapis philosophorum,* the philosophers' stone, is a symbolic "parallel of Christ" (Jung, *Alchemical Studies* 96, 320). See also Pet. 2.5: "Come, and let yourselves be built, as living stones, into a spiritual temple; become a holy priesthood, to offer spiritual sacrifices acceptable to God through Jesus Christ." Here, the reference to *sweat* is also significant. In fact, for the alchemists, "sweat meant dew" (Jung, *Mysterium Coniunctionis* 40). Accordingly, in the "Epistola ad Hermannum" (*Theatrum chemicum,* vol. V [1622] 894), the artifex says that, when redeemed, "'the body becomes moist, and gives forth a kind of bloody sweat after the putrefaction and mortification, that is, a Heavenly Dew, and this dew is called the Mercury of the Philosophers, or Aqua Permanens.'" (Jung cites this alchemical formula in *Mysterium Coniunctionis* 40n229). See also the note on *moist as the body that He has planned* given below. *The Water That Does Not Make the Hands Wet*

Lobate (LOW-bate) débris (DAY-bree) aprons: in this poem, piles of rounded, ice-rich, Martian rock débris. *Fixated on Mars*

Local Bubble: in the Milky Way Galaxy, a region in the Orion Arm—a great cavity approximately 300 light years across—that contains the Solar System. See the note on *The Orion Arm of the Milky Way* given below. *Local Bubble*

A loop recursive: here, the outside world conceived as a skein of active symbols, or timeless analogies, that twist and weave *self-referentially*—having been "looped around and directed at themselves"—in the ever-crafty, "holistic" human mind. Parsing Douglas R. Hofstadter's view that "It is the pattern inside the brain, not the brain itself, that makes us what we are," Paul Davies explores the "tangled hierarchy" of these "strange loops," along with the emergent features of the reflective self, in *God and the New Physics* (New York: Simon, 1983) 88-99. *Storyboard*

Made in the image of an image: Quoting Origen, the 3rd-century Christian theologian, Jung resolves this conundrum in *Aion* 37-38: "The *imago Dei* imprinted on the soul, not on the body, is an image of an image, 'for my soul is not directly the image of God, but is made after the likeness of the former image.' Christ, on the other hand, is the true image of God, after whose likeness our inner man is made invisible, incorporeal, incorrupt, and immortal." *Chain-Linked*

magnet in the beak: See James Gorman, "Study Sheds Light on How Birds Navigate by Magnetic Field," *The New York Times* 26 April 2012: 2 <www.nytimes.com>: "Efforts to understand the magnetic sense in birds have gone in several directions. Some researchers have offered evidence for chemical reactions in the eyes sensitive to magnetic signals, while others have looked at neurons in the beak that they thought contained minute amounts of magnetite, a mineral that is affected by magnetic fields." However, more recently, two researchers at the Baylor College of Medicine, Le-Qing Wu and David Dickman, have identified "cells in a pigeon's brain that are tuned to specific directions of the magnetic field." They also "have good, but not conclusive, evidence to suggest that the information that these cells are recording is coming from the bird's inner ear." *Fabricator*

magus: "a sorceror or [an] astrologer" ("Magus" [n.], def. 2)—here, either the ever-gestating NASA astronaut or "the inner, eternal man [hidden] in the shell of the outer, mortal man" (Jung, *Alchemical Studies* 150), the maker of this poem. *The Spear of Archytas*

Mandrake: i.e., the forked root of the mandrake (*Mandragora officinarum*), a medicinal plant formerly thought to possess occult powers because of its supposed resemblance to the human body—specifically, to a man standing upside down. In *Alchemical Studies,* Jung explains that "The idea that man is an inverted tree seems to have been current in the Middle Ages. [. . .] In Hindu literature the tree grows from above downwards, whereas in alchemy (at least according to the pictures) it grows from below upwards." However, "In East and West alike, the tree symbolizes a living process as well as a process of enlightenment" (312-14)—in fine, the work of both "[moral] transformation and [spiritual] renewal" (317). *Mastermind*

manna: the food given by God to the Israelites during the exodus from Egypt: "Israel called the food manna; it was white, like coriander seed, and it tasted like a wafer made with honey" (Exod. 16.31). *Here Be Dragons*

mare: a dark plain on the Earth's moon. The word is pronounced MAH-ray. *Gatekeeper; Here Be Dragons; Rebis; The Round Dance of the Stars*

Maria's Spagyric: i.e., the spagyric foetus, in alchemy "the renewed Mercurius," the symbolic androgyne that ascends into Heaven that it may become a spirit from a body and then descends to earth that it may become a body again. Cf. John 3.13: "'No one ever went up into heaven except the one who came down from Heaven, the Son of Man whose home is in heaven.'" See also Jung, *Psychology and Alchemy* 387, fig. 210: "The wind hath carried it in his belly," and the section on "Ascent and Descent" in Jung, *Mysterium Coniunctionis* 217-22. *Storyboard*

Maria, who do *you* say that I am? / An atom like a gram: The speaker addresses either the *Maria* of Gnostic tradition, the legendary "Prophetissa" and reputed "sister of Moses" (Jung, *Psychology and Alchemy* 401n169), or Mary, the Mother of God. One answer that *Maria* proffers is the *atom,* both "a transcendent entity" (Jung, *Aion* 249) and "the most elementary building-stone in the architecture of matter" (237). *Christ on Einstein's Tram*

mechatronic: pertaining to a fusion of various technologies—especially mechanical, electronic, and computer engineering—that aim to develop as well as to control intelligent machines. *Chain-Linked*

Meme: "a concept or behavior that spreads [like the transmission of genes] from person to person. Examples of memes include beliefs, fashions, stories, and phrases" typically dispersed "within local cultures or social groups" or through the Internet ("Meme," *TechTerms* 28 Nov. 2011 <www.techterms.com>). The popular term was coined in 1976 by the evolutionary biologist Richard Dawkins in *The Selfish Gene.* In this poem, the metaphorical "contraband" evokes such religious, scientific, and alchemical memes as "Shriven substance" and Endtime's "throne"; geometry's "tesseract" and relativity's "cone"; and the archetypal *Rubeus* ("The Red Man") and "animate stone." *Christ on Einstein's Train*

mercury: "the arcane substance" that the alchemists associated with Mercurius, "the light-bringing Nous, who knows the secret of transformation and of immortality" (Jung, *Mysterium Coniunctionis* 231). In alchemy, "Mercurius corresponds not only to Christ, but to the triune divinity in general" (Jung, *Alchemical Studies* 222). Not insignificantly, "In the scolia to the 'Tractatus aureus' the sign for Mercurius is a square inside a triangle surrounded by a circle (symbol of totality)" (224). *Ephesian Symbols*

metals: i.e., "the metals of the [Hermetic] Philosophers." However, the planetary names that enter the *opus* "refer ultimately not only to metals but, as every alchemist knew, to the (astrological) temperaments, that is, to psychic factors" (Jung, *Alchemical Studies* 275). Furthermore, as Jung suggests, the alchemists themselves may have discovered "that not only veins of ore are to be found in the mines, but also kobolds [helpful gnomes] and little metal men, and that there may be hidden in lead either a deadly demon or the dove of the Holy Ghost" (89). *Light of the Eye*

micro-fungi prized: See "Fungi in Space!" *Scientific American Blog Network* 7 June 2016 <blogs.scientificamerican.com>, where Jennifer Frazer explains that "fungi that live inside rocks in Antarctica have managed to survive a year and a half in low-Earth orbit under punishing Mars-like conditions" (2). Although few of the fungi "survived well enough to reproduce [. . .], at least a fraction did. Perhaps that is the material thing" (9). *Gateway*

milk skin that we smell: The fact that the skin of some newborn babies can *smell* like sweet *milk* is a prime example of "odor-dependent mother-infant bonding." See Johan N. Lundström et al., "Maternal status regulates cortical responses to the body odor of newborns," *Frontiers in Psychology* 5 Sept. 2013: 2 <www.frontiersin.org/articles>. *The Chariot of Aristotle's Wheels*

Minerals fluoresce in the presence of light: In 2008, after Chandrayaan-1, India's first moon probe, "entered lunar orbit and used its Moon Mineralogy Mapper to scan the surface," the X-ray signatures "of aluminium, magnesium, and silicon were detected [in the

Orientale basin]," a solar flare having "caused them to fluoresce" (David Whitehouse, *Space 2069: After Apollo: Back to the Moon, to Mars . . . and Beyond* [London: Icon Books, 2021] 55). *The Round Dance of the Stars*

Möbius' (MER-be-us) run: one of the many strange topologies of hyperspace—a continuous, one-sided geometric surface "created by twisting a strip of paper 180 degrees and then gluing the ends together." In effect, "outside and inside are identical" (Kaku, *Hyperspace* 60-61). The "Möbius strip" is named after its deviser, the nineteenth-century German mathematician A. F. Möbius. *Chain-Linked; Claim; Fixated on Mars; Here Be Dragons*

Moist *albedo*: a symbol of spiritual renewal, "the white state of innocence, which like the moon and a bride awaits the bridegroom" (Jung, *Mysterium Coniunctionis* 132). The medieval alchemists held that the moon "secretes the dew or sap of life" (131). *Here Be Dragons*

moist as the body that He has planned: In the alchemical *opus*, the "'body becomes moist, and gives forth a kind of bloody sweat, and this dew is called the Mercury of the Philosophers, or Aqua Permanens'" (Jung, *Mysterium Coniunctionis* 40n229), a fluid substance redolent of both the wingfooted Mercurius (the compensatory parallel of Christ) and "the demon-conquering moon" (140n239). See also the note on *Living stones exude a heavenly sweat* given above. *Fabricator*

Monad: not only the indivisible point—"the jot of the iota"—viewed as a Gnostic emblem of the totalistic man or woman (Jung, *Aion* 218), but also a basic unit of matter—a microcosm—that, according to the German philosopher and mathematician Gottfried Wilhelm von Leibnitz (1646-1716), mirrors the universe. *Containment and the Cosmic Edge; Gateway; Rebis*

moonchild in the wain: "a prefiguration of the [archetypal] self"—in alchemy, "the spagyric embryo conceived by the sun in [the] womb and belly" of the moon (Jung, *Mysterium Coniunctionis* 175-76). Here, the solar chariot of Apollo is recast as the lowly "wagon or cart" ("Wain" [n.], def.) of Christ, the Redeemer-King. *Light of the Eye*

The moon in transition raised to the sun: a symbolic picture of spiritual androgyny and the totalistic self. See Jung, *Psychology and Alchemy* 231-32: "the first main goal" of the alchemical process is the *albedo,* "highly prized by many alchemists as if it were the ultimate goal. It is the silver or moon condition, which still has to be raised to the sun condition. The *albedo* is, so to speak, the daybreak, but not till the *rubedo* is it sunrise." In effect, "The red and white are King and Queen, who may also celebrate their 'chymical wedding' at this stage" of the *opus,* i.e., the royal marriage of opposites that always occurs—not only in the emblematic Christ, the divine "bridegroom" (389), but also in His born-again believers—"outside the natural context" (464-65). See also 231, fig. 116: "Crowned hermaphrodite representing the union of king and queen, [standing] between the sun and moon trees." *The Moon in Transition Raised to the Sun*

Moriah's terrain: in Gen. 22.1-12, the land of Mount Moriah, where Abraham prepared to sacrifice his son Isaac. *Here Be Dragons*

Mother of the Night: Luna, the multi-natured moon that has "a double light, outside a feminine one but inside a masculine one which is hidden in it as a fire. Luna is really the mother of the sun, which means, psychologically, that the unconscious is pregnant with consciousness and gives birth to it. It is the night, which is older than the day." Evidently, for the alchemists, "From the darkness of the unconscious comes the light of illumination, the *albedo*. The opposites are contained in it *in potentia,* hence the hermaphroditism of the unconscious, its capacity for spontaneous and autochthonous [or innate] reproduction" (Jung, *Mysterium Coniunctionis* 177). *The Water That Does Not Make the Hands Wet*

Motion-captured: The speaker refers to the live movement of human subjects and its capture in humanoid robotics, which includes work for untethered humanoid teleoperation, robot locomotion, robot control, and human-robot interaction. See Nathan Miller, Odest Chadwicke Jenkins, Marcelo Kallmann, and Maja J. Mataric, "Motion Capture from Inertial Sensing for Untethered Humanoid Teleoperation," in *Proceedings of the IEEE-RAS International Conference on Humanoid Robotics* 24 June 2004: 3 <ieeexplore.ieee.org>. *Ephesian Symbols*

multiverse: a concept that derives from a cosmological theory advanced in 1957 by Hugh Everett, and later by Bryce DeWitt, both of whom argue that an infinite number of possible universes (including myriad copies of our local world) comprises but one part of physical reality (Kaku, *Hyperspace* 262-64). *The Path of Least Action*

my astronaut buoyed / Even as an orphan: the NASA wayfinder lifted up and inspirited ("Buoy" [vt.], def. 3) as either an embedded cyborg or a humanoid robot. See the note on *orphans* given below. *The Cusp of Skill*

My body begins to grow from the back. / Curved like a tail, or coat upon its rack: Cf. Kitzinger and Nilsson, *Being Born* 20: In the literal as well as the figurative early-stage embryo, "The [cell] ball now had a top end, big and round, that was going to be your head, and a bottom end that was thin and curved like a tail. Your body began to grow from the back and to join up at the front like a coat being zipped up." *The Heavenly Journey of the Shaman*

My fingers fully formed: See Kitzinger and Nilsson, *Being Born* 52-53: The human foetus having grown for eight months in the womb, its "fingernails were like tiny shells." *A Methane Snow*

my foam the driest: i.e., spacetime foam, the frothy, "sponge-like structure of the world canvas" (Davies, *Other Worlds* 96). Malcolm W. Browne upholds this theory in "Physicists Confirm Power of Nothing, Measuring Force of Quantum Foam," *The New York Times* 21 Jan. 1997, New Eng. ed.: C6: "We are all quantum fluctuations. [. . .] That's the origin of us all and of everything in the universe, not just dark matter." *The Round Dance of the Stars*

my robotic hand: a "smart glove" for astronauts, "a human-machine interface technology" designed for future "exploration of the moon, Mars—and possibly even other planets." In effect, the glove enables astronauts "to control drones or other robots [by] using simple hand gestures." See Idun Haugan, "Ground-breaking astronaut glove for exploring the moon and Mars," *Norwegian SciTech News* 19 Dec. 2019: 2 <norwegianscitechnews.com>. *Drilling on Mars*

mystagogues: interpreters of religious mysteries. *Chain-Linked; Christ on Einstein's Tram; Mastermind*

nascent in the dun: "a dull grayish brown" ("Dun" [n.], def. 1), like dust born "Behind the stars" (l. 8). *Gatekeeper*

navel's fold: here, the horizontal belly button *fold,* the remnant of the umbilical cord that connects the developing infant to the placenta. *The Water That Does Not Make the Hands Wet*

nebulae: clouds of interstellar gas or dust. According to the nebular hypothesis, "the solar system was once a nebula which condensed to form the sun and planets" ("Nebular Hypothesis," def.). *Channeling Hipparchus*

Neither male nor female nor *rebis* name: Cf. Gal. 3.28: "There is no such thing as Jew and Greek, slave and freeman, male and female; for you are all one person in Christ Jesus." In alchemy, the *rebis* is an androgyne, the "dual being born of the alchemical union of opposites" (masculine, feminine) and recognized "as a symbol of the self" (Jung, *Aion* 268). *Courtship*

Neptune's own Triton: The largest of Neptune's 13 moons, "Triton is unique among large satellites inasmuch as it orbits Neptune in a retrograde direction, so that[,] while Neptune rotates from west to east[,] Triton moves from east to west" (Moore, *Travellers in Space and Time* 67). *A Host-Star in Draco*

Nomads in the mare: wanderers on the surface of a lunar plain. *Here Be Dragons*

numinous: "having a deeply spiritual or mystical effect" ("Numinous" [adj.], def. 2). *The Man in the Moon*

obelisks: "tall, slender, four-sided stone pillar[s] tapering toward [their] pyramidal top[s]" ("Obelisk" [n.], def. 1). See the note on *Jachin and Boaz* given above. *Light of the Eye*

obol (AH-bul): an ancient Greek coin paid to Charon, the boatman of the underworld, who conveys "the wicked to everlasting torment and the good to a place of blessedness called the Elysian Fields." However, "Charon will receive into his boat only the souls of those upon whose lips the passage money was placed when they died and who were duly buried" (Hamilton, *Mythology* 39). By contrast, the Christian substitute for the *obol* is

Viaticum: the sacrament of the Holy Eucharist given to the shriven and the absolved—in this stanza, the reconciled penitent being either the *Rubeus,* the incarnate Savior, or the "animate stone," the symbolic "parallel of Christ" (Jung, *Alchemical Studies* 96), or both. *Christ on Einstein's Tram*

The offspring of the *rebis:* The speaker alludes to the reborn followers of Christ, the Risen Savior who is also the crowned hermaphrodite, a symbol of the holistic self. *Extract of the Macrocosm*

omniverse: not only a universe that is four-dimensional, but also, in current physical cosmology, an infinity of universes—the conglomeration of all possible worlds. *Chain-Linked; Extract of the Macrocosm; Light of the Eye; Rebis*

omphalos: the mid-point or navel of the earth—Golgotha; according to an ancient Christian tradition, both the hill where Adam was buried and the very spot where Christ was crucified. See Jung, *Mysterium Coniunctionis* 388-89. *Evangelist; The Smoke-Hole of the Tent; The Woman in the Moon*

On shuttle stacks loaded, boosters that rise: the "classic" stacks of booster rockets and external fuel tanks that helped launch NASA's shuttles into space. See Brian Dunbar, "Shuttle Stack Construction Marks Latest Milestone," *NASA* 12 Apr. 2013: 1 <www.nasa.gov>. Last updated 17 Aug. 2017. *The Spear of Archtyas*

On the retina a patchwork of tints: a paradox that Jonathan Miller unravels in *The Body in Question* 42: "our senses introduce us to a world, and not just to a kaleidoscope of sensations. The visual world, for example, is not just a patchwork of tints—although that is all there is on our retina. [. . .] In the very act of entering consciousness, sensations are somehow made up into scenery and we experience them as objects in the world. But this doesn't happen automatically. The mind has to make a guess about the identity of what it sees, hears, or feels, and the odds are determined by all sorts of hints and hot tips." In sum, each "imaginary picture" that we "improvise" appears to be—like the Cheshire cat in *Alice's Adventures in Wonderland*—both there and not there. *Spacetime's Wight*

opus: the *work* of redemption as a divine *art* (Jung, *Psychology and Alchemy* 306, 313)—in effect, as a *human*-centered transformative process: in alchemy, of lead into gold, and later, in the Gnostic tradition, and also in Jungian psychology, of the psyche, i.e., the "living" mind, into the integrated self (Jung, *Alchemical Studies* 328). However, Jung reminds us that the "*opus alchymicum,* in spite of its chemical aspects, was always understood as a kind of rite after the manner of an *opus divinum.* For this reason the Hungarian alchemist Melchior Cibinensis, at the beginning of the sixteenth century, could still represent it in the form of a Mass, since long before this the *filius* or *lapis philosophorum* had been regarded as an allegory of Christ" (*Alchemical Studies* 123). In other words, the "Son of Man" had become a synonym for the holistic self (*Psychology and Alchemy* 208). *The Chariot of Aristotle's Wheels; Circumambient; Extract of the Macrocosm; The Woman in the Moon*

Or *blue silicone sole*: an alternate image that captures the footprint left in the lunar soil at Tranquility Base—specifically, "the blue silicone sole of the lunar overshoe" designed by Richard Ellis, "a model maker" for ILC Industries, and worn by the NASA astronaut Eugene Cernan during the Apollo 17 mission. See John Branch, "One Small Step for Man, One Big Step for Moon Boots," *The New York Times* 17 July 2019: 2 <nytimes.com>. (In this line [4], the speaker emphasizes Photo 8 from an insert-essay—"Boot, Left, Lunar Overshoe, Cernan, Apollo 17, Flown" <airandspace.si.edu>—given in Branch's "One Small Step . . ." 5). See also the note on *Coheir's silicone sole* given above and *Or rungs of a ladder* given below. *Christ on Einstein's Tram*

or else a pair: a Gnostic conundrum. The speaker refers not only to the divided participants in the agony of the Cross—Christ, the principle of preconscious masculine spirituality, and Sophia, the embodiment of both Wisdom and the afflicted soul (Jung, *Alchemical Studies* 335-37)—but also to the selfsame "pairs of opposites [that] constitute the phenomenology of the paradoxical self" (Jung, *Mysterium Coniunctionis* 6). In other words, the double quaternity "stands for a totality, for something that is at once heavenly and earthly, spiritual or corporeal, and is found in the 'Indian Ocean,' that is to say in the unconscious. It is without doubt the Microcosm, the mystical Adam and bisexual Original Man in his prenatal state, as it were, when he is identical with the unconscious. Hence in Gnosticism the 'Father of All' is described not only as masculine and feminine (or neither), but as Bythos, the abyss" (11). *The Heavenly Journey of the Shaman*

Or, in the slit, the paradox that saves: a reference to the residual uncertainty that is "apparently an inherent property of the microworld" (Davies, *Other Worlds* 62). Thus, in the famous two-slit experiment, "we must conclude that *potential* electron paths thread through both slits in the screen, and that in some strange way those paths that are not followed still influence the behaviour of the actual path." In short, it is "an interference of probability. [. . .] Phrased differently, the alternative worlds that could have existed, but did not come to do so, still influence the world that does exist, like the fading grin of the Cheshire cat" (67) in *Alice's Adventures in Wonderland*. *Storyboard*

The Orion Arm of the Milky Way: In Greek mythology, *Orion* is a hunter whom the Moon goddess Artemis loves but accidentally kills. "After his death he was placed in heaven as a constellation" (Hamilton, *Mythology* 297). See also Engelbrektson, *Stars, Planets, and Galaxies* 24: "[Orion [. . .] consists of seven bright stars that outline the figure," three of which "represent his belt." In our corner of the *Milky Way* Galaxy, the Sun is located in the *Orion Arm*. *Local Bubble*

Or metaverses tear in Saturn's lair: In cosmology, a metaverse is a "spectrum" of possible universes (Brian Greene, *The Hidden Reality: Parallel Universes and the Deep Laws of the Cosmos* (New York: Vintage-Random, 2011) 4. Greene explains the *tear* in the *metaverses* with a vivid analogy in *The Elegant Universe:* "If you stretch a rubber membrane, sooner or later it will tear. This simple fact has inspired numerous physicists over the years to ask whether the same might be true of the spatial fabric making up the universe. That is, can the fabric of space rip apart, or is this merely a misguided notion that arises from taking the rubber analogy too seriously?" Greene proceeds to demonstrate that "a new formulation of physics that goes beyond Einstein's classical theory [of general relativity] and [that] incorporates quantum physics might [indeed] show that rips, tears, and mergers of the spatial fabric can occur" (263). In the poem, the speaker also refers to Saturn, the ambivalent Roman god of both generation and dissolution. His *lair* is Creation itself. *Claim*

Or perhaps a riff or only a reed: The speaker compares himself to "a constantly repeated musical phrase" ("Riff" [n.], def. 1) and, metonymically, to the sound of the nai [nigh], a revived, ancient Arabic reed flute. *Extract of the Macrocosm*

orphans: ever-evolving humanoid robots, in the [Slavic] root sense of the latter word, *orb-*, i.e., *separated from [the] group* like a child without parents. *The Cusp of Skill; Ephesian Symbols*

Orpheus: the legendary Greek poet-musician who "took the fearsome journey to the underworld" (Hamilton, *Mythology* 104). "There was no limit to his power when he played and sang. No one and nothing could resist him" (103). *Ephesian Symbols*

Or rungs of a ladder: an alternate reading of this line (4). See John Branch, "One Small Step for Man, One Big Step for Moon Boots," *The New York Times* 17 July 2019: 2 <www.nytimes.com>: "On July 20, 1969, the Apollo 11 astronaut Buzz Aldrin took a step forward, backed up, then took a photograph. What he left behind on the moon and captured for the rest of us on Earth remains remarkable in its simplicity and timeless in its evocation. [. . .] Mr. Aldrin's footprint is about an inch deep—enough to cast a shadow from the dim sunlight over his right shoulder. It is straight on the sides and rounded at the toes and the heel, the shape of a racetrack. It is filled with lines, like rungs of a ladder, formed by eight flat, straight-edged ribs." See the note on *Coheir's silicone sole* and on *Or blue silicone sole* given above. *Christ on Einstein's Tram*

Our brain cells vacillate lest we forget: In *Windows on the Mind,* according to Erich Harth, the word *reflection* "appears to be a very apt description of thought." Thus, the cerebral cortex "literally reflects," i.e., "bounces back images that have impinged on it, producing new and modified inputs for itself" (102). In fact, "The brain is the epitome of a self-referent system. My self is forever imaging itself and changing in response to the image. It can never quite catch up with itself" (215). *Bootstrap*

Ouroboros (oar-oh-*boar*-ahs): a loop phenomenon: the snake that bites its own tail—in alchemy, not only a self-described circle, the *opus* that "proceeds from the one and leads back to the one" (Jung, *Psychology and Alchemy* 293 and fig. 147), but also a symbol of totality. *Claim; Extract of the Macrocosm; The Heavenly Journey of the Shaman; Here Be Dragons; Psalter; Rite; Scion; Spacetime's Wight; The Water That Does Not Make the Hands Wet*

Out of nothing he grew: In *Perfect Symmetry: The Search for the Beginning of Time* (New York: Simon, 1985), Heinz R. Pagels remarks that, according to the 1984 Stephen Hawking-James Hartle model of the origin of the universe, "The nothingness 'before' the creation of the universe is the most complete void that we can imagine—no space, time or matter existed. It is a world without place, without duration or eternity, without number—it is what the mathematicians call 'the empty set.' Yet this unthinkable void converts itself into the plenum of existence—a necessary consequence of physical laws" (347). *Claim*

Palm trees: In the Bible, the palm-tree is, like the terebinth, a sacred tree. See Psalm 92.12-15: "The righteous flourish like a palm-tree, they grow tall as a cedar on Lebanon; / planted as they are in the house of the Lord, they flourish in the courts of our God, / vigorous in old age like trees full of sap, luxuriant, wide-spreading, / eager to declare that the Lord is just, the Lord my rock, in whom there is no unrighteousness." See also the note on *terebinths* given below. *Chain-Linked*

Pandora's jar: In Greek mythology, Pandora is "the source of all misfortune," not because of her "wicked nature," but because of "her curiosity." Thus, "The gods presented her with a box [in this poem a *jar*] into which each had put something harmful, and forbade her to open it." Nevertheless, "She *had* to know what was in the box. One day she lifted the lid—and out flew plagues innumerable, sorrow and mischief [. . .]. In terror Pandora clapped the lid down, but too late. One good thing, however, was there—Hope, [. . .] and it remains to this day mankind's sole comfort in misfortune" (Hamilton, *Mythology* 70, 72). *Cat's Eye*

Panspermia: "a theory holding that the seeds of life diffuse naturally through outer space" ("Panspermia" [n.], def.)—in this poem, transported by comets. *Gateway*

parsecs: A parsec (*par*[allax] + *sec*[ond]) is a unit of astronomical length equivalent to 3.26 light years or to 206,265 times the distance from the earth to the sun ("Parsec" [n.], def.). *Courtship; Ephesian Symbols*

Particle colliders: atom smashers—e.g., Hadron and Tevatron, enormous *particle* accelerators in which beams of protons and antiprotons are made to collide at the near-speed of light in order that scientists may probe, at infinitesimal scales, the structure of matter, space, and time. *Evangelist*

pasteboard: a Bristol-board—in England, "a stiff material made of layers of paper pasted together" ("Pasteboard" [n.], def. 1) and used by artists and printers. *Scion*

the path of least action: Bob Toben, "in conversation" with the physicists Jack Sarfatti and Fred Wolf, defines this mind-altering concept in *Space-Time and Beyond*. Thus, the goal-directed path of least action is "'ordinary' reality" fixed and patterned according to Newtonian physics. However, another view—that of quantum mechanics—suggests that, since reality is a function of our "participation with an indefinite number" of probabilistic paths (95), we may extend the "infinite lattice" of *least action* strands that constitute our perception of the cosmos, even as we expand our consciousness. In other words, the search for holistic order in the universe can lead us, through "star-like acts of awareness," from one chance-varied *path of least action* to another (159). *The Path of Least Action*

peacock: "an early Christian symbol for the Redeemer" (Jung, *Psychology and Alchemy* 419), since its "combination of all colors" signifies wholeness (223). According to

Chevalier and Gheerbrant, in medieval literature, because it "spreads its tail in the shape of a wheel," the peacock "evokes the starry sky" and hence is also "a [solar] sign of immortality" (*The Penguin Dictionary of Symbols* 741-42). *Bootstrap*

perilune: the point nearest to the center of the moon in the orbit of a spacecraft. *Rebis*

Phoebe: In Greek mythology, "As Phoebus was the Sun," *Phoebe* "was the Moon" (Hamilton, *Mythology* 31), a goddess also called Artemis and Selene. *The Man in the Moon; Scout*

Photons: "messengers [. . .] between particles of matter" (Davies, *The Mind of God* 207), each of them being "massless" (208) and conveying the "smallest bundle of light" (Greene, *The Elegant Universe* 419). *Courtship; Rite; The Round Dance of the Stars; Schrödinger's Cat; The Spear of Archytas*

pine trees: In the worship of Cybele during the decline of the Roman Empire, "The pine symbolized the body of the god [the self-castrated Attis] who died and was restored to life again" (Chevalier and Gheerbrant, *The Penguin Dictionary of Symbols* 756). In this poem, the Aleppo (Syria) *pine* to which the speaker refers is also known as the Jerusalem *pine* and is often used as a Christmas tree, the evergreen that, even today, Christians associate with both the Son of God and the Tree of Life in Genesis 2.9. *The Woman in the Moon*

pixels: The speaker cites one source of the cosmos: "the basic unit or picture element that makes up the image displayed on a video screen" ("Pixel" [n.], def.). *Storyboard*

Planet Nine: a celestial body, but hypothetical. Through mathematical modeling and computer simulations, Konstantin Batygin and Mike Brown, Caltech astronomers, "have found evidence of a giant planet tracing a bizarre, highly elongated orbit in the outer solar system." The object, which they nicknamed *Planet Nine,* "has a mass about 10 times that of Earth and orbits about 20 times farther from the sun on average than does Neptune (which orbits the sun at an average distance of 2.8 billion miles). In fact, it would take this new planet between 10,000 and 20,000 years to make just one full orbit around the sun." See Kim Fesenmeier, "Caltech Researchers Find Evidence of a Real Ninth Planet," *Caltech* 26 Jan. 2016: 1 <www.caltech.edu>. *Gateway*

pleats: in speculative fiction, folded space that results in faster-than-light travel. *Storyboard*

plover: the golden *plover* (*Charadrius pluvialis*), a shorebird that "gets its name from the fact that it lives in a [. . .] 'crack in the earth'" and that its song "heralds the rain" (Jung, *Symbols of Transformation* 289). In the *Metamorphoses,* Ovid depicts the *plover* as a "soul-bird" that flew up into the air from the tree-covered body of Kaineus [KEYE-noose], the "invulnerable" Lapith hero overcome in the battle with the cunning Centaurs. *Splitting the Earth with a Straight Foot*

Plumules that scatter, coverts that decay: The speaker refers to the feathers of the peacock, "with its crest of plumules and long, brightly colored upper tail coverts that can be spread out like a fan and have rainbow-colored, eyelike spots" ("Peacock" [n.], def. 1). In *Psychology and Alchemy,* Jung remarks that the peacock was "an early Christian symbol for the Redeemer" (419), since its "combination of all colors" signifies wholeness (223). *Bootstrap*

Pneuma: either "a wind-breath or spirit" (Jung, *Symbols of Transformation* 316) or "the Son of God, who descends into matter and then frees himself from it in order to bring healing and salvation to all souls" (Jung, *Psychology and Alchemy* 301). "The cabalistic idea of God pervading the world in the form of soul-sparks (*scintillae*) and the Gnostic idea of the Spinther (spark) are similar" (301n26). *Ephesian Symbols*

Pneumatic: "having to do with the spirit or soul" ("Pneumatic" [adj.], def. 3). See 1 Cor. 15.45: "Scripture [Gen. 2.7] says, 'The first man, Adam, became an animate being' [i.e., a living soul], whereas the last Adam [Jesus Christ, the all-inclusive Son of God] has become a life-giving spirit." *The Cusp of Skill*

The podium on which Our Savior stands: Cf. Jung, *Mysterium Coniunctionis* 206: "The four gospels form, as it were, a quaternary podium [a raised platform] on which the Redeemer stands." See also Jung's thesis that the relationship between Christianity and alchemy is "a process of assimilation between revealed truth and knowledge of nature" that has proven—for both religion and psychology—not only enriching but also "highly desirable" (325). *Ephesian Symbols*

point: According to Johann Christoph Steeb, a Renaissance alchemist, "The point is most akin to the nature of light, and light is a *simulacrum Dei*" (Jung, *Alchemical Studies* 151)—i.e., a trace or a semblance or an image of God. See also *Mysterium Coniunctionis* 45, where Jung quotes another alchemist, John Dee, Steeb's contemporary: "'Things and beings have their first origin in the point and the monad.'" *Scintilla's Scan*

Polaris: the Polestar, i.e., the North Star, "the point around which everything turns" and hence "a symbol of the self" (Jung, *Psychology and Alchemy* 188). *Channeling Hipparchus; Schrödinger's Cat*

The Pole in the sky: See the note on *Polaris* given above. In alchemy, "Mercurius is the world-soul, and the Pole is its heart" (Jung, *Psychology and Alchemy* 188). *A Methane Snow*

Pours into a mill in the form of scrolls / Upon cloven tongues the Word that He doles: The speaker refers to the Day of Pentecost, when the Holy Spirit appeared to the regenerated faithful—His believer-priests—"like flames of fire, dispersed [or divided] among them and resting on each one," and thereafter "they began to talk in other tongues, as the Spirit gave them power of utterance" (Acts 2.2.). See also "The 'Mill of the Host,'" fig. 158, in Jung, *Psychology and Alchemy* 307, where "The Word, in the form of scrolls, is poured into a mill by the four evangelists, to reappear as the Infant Christ in the chalice." According to Jung, the latter "myth-picture" implies that "redemption is a work" (306). *Trapeze*

prefigured at the sign of the Ram: See Jung, *Aion* 90: "to the extent that Christ was regarded as the first aeon, it would be clear to anyone acquainted with astrology that he was born as the first fish of the Pisces era, and was doomed to die as the last ram [or, in Hebrew astrology, lamb] of the declining Aries era." *Scout*

Present in the psyche: Cf. Jung, *Psychology and Alchemy* 185: "In the case of the modern man, who has no religious assumptions at all," it is inevitable that "the [Gnostic] Anthropos or Poimen [the symbolic shepherd] figure should emerge," since the archetype of the divine original man "is present in his own psyche" as "an autonomous psychological fact." *Circumambient*

Primordial atoms that ravel smart: The speaker refers not only to the 19th-century notion that *atoms* are nothing more than inner-directed, holistic spherules of force, but also to the current chip-based system of *smart* dust: "nanostructured flakes of porous silicon" that can self-assemble, mimic particles, and then spread into the atmosphere even as they collect and monitor computational data. See "Smart Dust," *UCSD Sailor Research Group* 13 Sept. 2009 <http://sailorgroup.ucsd.edu/research/smartdust>. *The Path of Least Action*

projectile like a stone: in alchemy, the philosophers' *stone* taken as a symbol of the unified self, i.e., "of the inner Christ, of God in man" (Jung, *Alchemical Studies* 96). *Scion*

Prophetissa: in Gnostic tradition, Maria the Jewess, the storied (3rd-century) prophetess, alchemist, and sister of Moses. *The Round Dance of the Stars*

proximal: here, an anatomical term: "situated nearest the center of the body or nearest the point of attachment of a muscle, limb, etc." ("Proximal" [adj.], def. 2). *Scion*

psalter: "a version of the Psalms for use in religious services" ("Psalter" [n.], def.). *Psalter*

Puer aeternus: the divine boy who "can strike no roots in the world" because he "is, as it were, only a dream of the mother, an ideal whom she soon takes back into herself, as we can see from the Near East 'son-gods' like Tammuz, Attis, Adonis, and Christ" (Jung, *Symbols of Transformation* 258). However, in alchemical literature, because he committed no sin, the *puer* becomes—paradoxically—not only "the quadripartite original man" (Jung, *Psychology and Alchemy* 133), but also "the unique historical reality" (185) of both "light and Logos" (331), i.e., a being clothed and quickening in the person of the Pauline Christ, "the philosophic Word" (374) made flesh. *Ephesian Symbols; Extract of the Macrocosm; A Methane Snow; Splitting the Earth with a Straight Foot*

a pup of celestial hue: in alchemy, the duplex Mercurius in his guise as Logos [the Person of the Son as the Word of God], whereby "the inner man" confronts "the animal man" (Jung, *Alchemical Studies* 90), the "puppy of celestial hue" (232n18). *Light of the Eye*

A quality, not a hypostasis: Jung suggests that the self "is a union of opposites par excellence" since "it combines uniqueness with eternity and the individual with the universal" (Jung, *Psychology and Alchemy* 19). However, in its "bewildering profusion of semblances" (181), these are its "'metaphysical' attributes," i.e., "qualities predicated by the unconscious" (105), not its divine "essence" or "underlying essential nature" ("Hypostasis" [n.]. def. 3). *Psalter*

quantum eyes: With this phrase the speaker encapsulates Goethe's belief in "the life-giving powers of light," even as he underscores the visible light that passes through the human eyeball. Thus, "Light, ever active, created the eye. It sculpted an organ suited to itself, like the streaming water shaping the stones over and through which it flows. Had light not 'seen' man, we should never have seen the light" (Zajonc, *Catching the Light* 341). *Rite*

A quantum of light: i.e., a photon—in the *quantum* theory of matter, a pulse or packet that contains "a given [fixed] quantity of energy" (Davies, *Other Worlds* 32) and that functions as both "wave of probability" (64) and particle. *Evangelist*

Quaternity's startlement: See *Aion* 224n7, where Jung remarks that "The circle has the character of wholeness because of its 'perfect' form; the quaternity, because four is the minimum number of parts into which the circle may be naturally divided." Thus, "the quaternity of Christ [. . .] is exemplified by the cross symbol" (204). Here, of course, the speaker responds to an unexpected embodiment of the God-image: "Adam before the Fall" (39). *Rebis*

Quicksilver: in alchemy, a metal that is not only liquid like water (Jung, *Alchemical Studies* 207) and concrete like silver (Jung, *The Archetypes and the Collective Unconscious* 312), but also "penetrating like spirit-substance" (*Alchemical Studies* 297) and, of course, duplicitous like Mercurius, the latter consummate trickster being both "the father of all metals" (235) and an image of the ambivalent self (237). *Ephesian Symbols; The Round Dance of the Stars*

Quicksilver scion: here, Mercurius (or the alchemical Hermes), "who possessed a double nature, being a chthonic god of revelation and also the spirit of quicksilver, for which reason he was represented as a hermaphrodite" (Jung, *Psychology and Alchemy* 65). *The Round Dance of the Stars*

The quilted universe: i.e., the quilted *multi*verse, an infinite *universe* composed, like a gigantic quilt, of patchwork parallel worlds (Greene, *The Hidden Reality* 355). *Splitting the Earth with a Straight Foot*

qwiff: a quantum wave function that describes "the probability of an observation and not the actual observation" (Fred Alan Wolf, *Taking the Quantum Leap* [New York: Harper, 1981] 170). An offshoot of wave-particle duality, qwiffs "are called functions because they are functional, which means [that] they depend on things for their operation"—on space and time (186). In effect, "Qwiffs represent what *could* take place in reality." Nevertheless, as ghostly, quantum-jumping particles, "Qwiffs predict with *uncertainty* [emphasis added] the behavior of matter" (219). Thus, according to Wolf, it is the human perceiver who activates the *qwiff*—i.e., turns it on and off—and, with each observation, collapses the wave of probability into reality. *Ephesian Symbols*

A rack for his tools: See the photo of the Apollo 12 landing site, "in a flat mare region," in Kerrod, *Space Walks* 36-37. "In the picture [the astronaut] Charles Conrad is unloading the experimental equipment from a bay in the lunar module. By his feet is a rack for the tools [that] he and fellow moonwalker Alan Bean need [in order] to start some lunar 'gardening.'" *Waxing in Luna into the Nature of the Sun*

The radical moisture that Venus doled: not only "the prima materia, which is the original chaos and the sea," i.e., the unconscious (Jung, *Mysterium Coniunctionis* 9), but also an active sun-substance, the balsam that is both a "daemonic principle" (Jung, *Mysterium Coniunctionis* 94) and a "miraculous power" (95) and is thus linked to the ambivalent Sol no less than to the double-dealing Mercurius. Clearly, for the alchemists, the sun is "an instrument in the physiological and psychological drama of [the eternal] return to the prima materia, the death that must be undergone if man is to get back to the original condition of the simple elements" and thereby "attain the incorrupt nature of the pre-worldly paradise" (99). *The Water That Does Not Make the Hands Wet*

Ramjets: constant acceleration starships capable of interstellar travel, a design proposed in 1960 by Robert W. Bussard and augmented later by other astrophysicists. *Drilling on Mars*

Reality before us, nets that flow / Evoke from each captive treasures that grow / Both tall and thin, like Einstein's tram, so slow / We twine such skein as senses overthrow: In *The Ascent of Man,* Bronowski explains that, according to the Principle of Relativity, "things change shape. [. . .] what you see and what I see is relative to each of us, that is, to our place and speed." Thus, in Illustration 120, "The observer in the stationary tram sees the houses undistorted." However, in the moving tram, he "sees them [as] tall and thin" because the tram is traveling at high speeds. Of course, as Bronowski indicates, speeding clocks run down: "if I rode on a beam of light, time would suddenly come to an end for me. And that must mean that, as I approach the speed of light (which is what I am going to simulate in this tram), I am alone in my box of time and space, which is more and more departing from the norms around me" (248-51). *Bootstrap*

***Rebis* (*ray*-bis or *ray*-beese):** a basic alchemical symbol. "[C]ompounded of two parts and therefore frequently hermaphroditic as an amalgam of Sol and Luna," the *rebis* "depicts the consciousness-transcending fact [that] we call the self" (Jung, *Psychology and Alchemy* 202). *Chain-Linked; Christ on Einstein's Tram; Circumambient; Courtship; The Cusp of Skill; Extract of the Macrocosm; The Heavenly Journey of the Shaman; Local Bubble; The Man in the Moon; The Moon in Transition Raised to the Sun; Rebis; Schrödinger's Cat; Scout; The Spear of Archytas*

Reborn in the sun: See Jung, *Psychology and Alchemy* 84: "the sun is an antique symbol that is still close to us." In fact, "early Christians had some difficulty in distinguishing" the rising sun from Christ, the implication being that, in the modern world, some "regressive" dreamers are still "sun-worshippers." *Fabricator*

red dwarfs: stars "cooler on [their] surface, smaller, and of fainter luminosity than the sun" ("Red Dwarf," def.). See also Lee Mohon, "Assessing the Habitability of Planets Around Old Red Dwarfs," *NASA* 30 Oct. 2020: 2 <www.nasa.gov>, where Kevin France, a professor in the Department of Astrophysical and Planetary Sciences at the University of Colorado in Boulder, reminds us that "Red dwarfs are the most numerous types of stars, and [that] their small sizes make them favorable for studying orbiting planets," especially "what the prospects are for habitable planets around red dwarfs [. . .], older red dwarfs in particular." *A Host-Star in Draco*

repairs cracked stringers: i.e., the damaged support beams in the space shuttle Discovery's external fuel tank. See Steven Siceloff, "Technicians Use Scanners to Survey External Tank," along with the accompanying image: "Technicians spray foam insulation on space shuttle Discovery's external tank to cover [. . .] repaired stringers," *NASA – Space Shuttle* 23 Nov. 2010: 1-2 <nasa.com>. *The Moon in Transition Raised to the Sun*

Resorb such flakes as migrate and then mill, / Like Oldowan scratch marks: See Erin Wayman, "The Origin of Stone Tools," *Smithsonian Magazine* 1 Oct. 2012: 3-4 <www.smithsonianmag.com>: "The oldest-known type of stone tools are stone flakes and the rock cores from which these flakes were removed. Presumably used for chopping and scraping, these tools are called Oldowan, named for Tanzania's Olduvai Gorge, where they were first recognized." In fact, "anthropologists suspect that by 2.6 million years ago hominids had been making stone tools for thousands of years." *The Cusp of Skill*

retort: the "wonder-working" Hermetic vessel, in this poem not only a melting furnace that contains "the arcane substance" to be transformed (Jung, *Alchemical Studies* 72), but also "a uterus of spiritual renewal or rebirth" (73). *Mastermind*

ringers: the plural form of *ringer:* either "any substitute" or "a person or thing very closely resembling another" ("Ringer"[2] [n.], defs. 1b and 1c) or, simply enough, a robot clone. *The Moon in Transition Raised to the Sun*

Robonaut: NASA's robotic astronaut, a "state-of-the-art humanoid" designed for space travel. "Outside the spacecraft, it will perform its tasks under the control of a human operator at a tele-presence console" (Peter Menzel and Faith D'Aluisio, *Robo sapiens: Evolution of a New Species* (Cambridge: MIT P, 2000) 129. See also Julia Badger and Ron Diftler, "Robonaut 2," *Robonaut–NASA,* 20 Sept. 2019 <robonaut.jsc.nasa.gov>), a useful update on the subject. Thus, having been "upgraded by the addition of two climbing manipulators ('legs')," *Robonaut* 2 (R2) is now "capable of speeds more than four times faster" than *Robonaut* 1 (R1), "is more compact [and] more dexterous," and includes such advanced features as "series elastic joint technology, extended finger and thumb travel, miniaturized 6-axis load cells, redundant force sensing, [and also] ultra high-speed joint controllers" (1-2). *Bootstrap; The Cusp of Skill*

Robonaut's glove: "a robotic glove, called RoboGlove," developed originally "as a grasp-assist device" for Robonaut 2 (R2) and later for human astronauts "performing skilled hand movements during Extravehicular Activity (EVA)—or spacewalks" (Kristine Rainey, "Robonaut's Potential Shines in Multiple Space, Medical and Industrial Applications," NASA 12 Nov. 2015: 1 <www.nasa.gov>). *Claim; Evangelist*

A rocky giant, a version of Earth, / Its host-star in Draco: Astronomers have found that "the extrasolar planet Kepler-10c, once thought to be a giant, is actually a 'mega-Earth.' Kepler-10c was originally spotted by NASA's Kepler Space Telescope in May 2011. The planet lies in the constellation Draco, about 564 light-years away, and circles its host-star, Kepler-10, once every 45 days." However, "Kepler-10c has a mass about 17 times that of Earth—far more than expected. This shows that the exoplanet must have a dense composition of rocks and other solids." Not insignificantly, the Kepler-10 system "is about 11 billion years old, which means [that] it formed less than 3 billion years after the Big Bang." Thus, according to Dr. Dimitar Sasselov, a professor from The Harvard-Smithsonian Center for Astrophysics, "Kepler 10-c has positive implications for life. [. . .] Finding Kepler 10-c tells us that rocky planets could form much earlier than we thought. And if you can make rocks, you can make life." See "Kepler-10c: Astronomers Find Mega-Earth," *Sci-News* 2 June 2014: 1-3 <www.sci-news.com>. *A Host-Star in Draco*

rook: In alchemical texts, the raven or *rook* symbolizes the *nigredo* or blackness—"the initial state [in the transformation] either present from the beginning as a quality of the *prima materia*, the chaos or *massa confusa*, or else produced by the separation (*solutio, separatio, divisio, putrefactio*) of the elements" (Jung, *Psychology and Alchemy* 230). *The Path of Least Action*

rotundum: in alchemy, the "round, original form" of "the spiritual, inner, and complete man" (Jung, *Mandala Symbolism* 9-10). *Rebis*

The Round Dance of the Stars: Jung explicates this concept in *Psychology and Western Religion:* "Since olden times the circle with a centre has been a symbol for the Deity, illustrating the wholeness of God incarnate: the single point in the centre and the series of points constituting the circumference." Not surprisingly, then, "Ritual circumambulation often bases itself quite consciously on the cosmic picture of the starry heavens revolving, [i.e.,] on the 'dance of the stars,' an idea that is still preserved in the comparison of the twelve disciples with the zodiacal constellations, [and] also in the depictions of the zodiac that are sometimes found in churches, in front of the altar or on the roof of the nave. [. . .] At all events, the aim and effect of the solemn round dance is to impress upon the mind the image of the circle and the centre and the relation of each point along the periphery to that centre. Psychologically this arrangement is equivalent to a mandala and is thus a symbol of the self, the point of reference not only of the individual ego but of all those who are of like mind or who are bound together by fate" (172). See the note on *I will be wounded* placed above and on *To each and all it is given to dance* placed below. *The Round Dance of the Stars*

the *rubedo*: i.e., the reddening, both the final stage in the alchemical *opus* and "the continuation of [the] albedo," the whiteness synonymous with the Light of Resurrection. "That is why they are often connected to each other, like the White Queen and the Red King. [. . .] In the eastern philosophies [the] rubedo corresponds with the formation of the 'diamond body,' [. . .] the pure and permanent Stone of the Philosophers" (Dirk Gillabel, "Alchemy 1.6: Rubedo-Redness," *Soul Guidance* 18 <www.soulguidance.com>. Accessed 17 Sept. 2017. See also the note on *stone* given below. *Schrödinger's Cat*

rubeous tincture: in alchemy, sulphur or fire, that is, "ruddy and burning" Sol, "the active substance of the sun or of the gold" (Jung, *Mysterium Coniunctionis* 93nn9-10). See the note on *Like the redness of the Egyptian Set* and on the *rubedo* given above and also the comment on *Rubeus* given below. *The Water That Does Not Make the Hands Sweat*

Rubeus: the red man (the *vir rubeus*) or the red slave (the *servus rubicundus*) who unites with the white woman (the *femina alba* or *mulier candida*), "a union that must refer to the royal marriage of Sol and Luna" (Jung, *Mysterium Coniunctionis* 147), the "traditional pair" of the alchemical *coniunctio* (131n183). In modern terminology, this "synthesis" of male and female "corresponds to the psychological idea of the self," i.e., the *lapis* [the living philosophical stone], both "the product of conscious and unconscious" (371) and a symbol of the incarnate Christ. Jung adds that, because the *lapis* "is itself androgynous, [. . .] there is no need" for another *coniunctio* (371-72). *Christ on Einstein's Tram*

rust: See Jung, *Psychology and Alchemy* 159: "In the alchemical view rust, like verdigris [its green, or greenish-blue, coating], is the metal's sickness. But at the same time this leprosy is [. . .] the basis for the preparation of the philosophical gold." Thus, "The paradoxical remark of Thales [c. 624-c. 546 BC] that the rust alone gives the coin its true value is a kind of alchemical quip, which at bottom only says that there is no light without shadow and no psychic wholeness without imperfection. To round itself out, life calls not for perfection but for completeness; and for this the 'thorn in the flesh' is needed, the suffering of defects without which there is no progress and no ascent." *Cat's-Eye*

Sabaean a temple inside a square: "The ground-plan of the Sabaean temple of Mercurius was a triangle inside a square" (Jung, *Alchemical Studies* 224). Here, the triangle represents "body, spirit, and soul" (Jung, *Psychology and Alchemy* 125n41), even as the *square* evokes "the plan of a *building"* (126), a symbol of both the philosophic Mercurius and the Christ-centered astronaut himself. *The Heavenly Journey of the Shaman*

A sacred fig-tree: in this lyric, the "imposing" banyan tree. According to Chevalier and Gheerbrant, throughout Southeast Asia, banyans are not only "homes for countless spirits"—they "also symbolize immortality and higher knowledge and were the trees under which the Buddha preferred to sit when he taught his disciples" (*The Penguin Dictionary of Symbols* 377). Even Jesus was partial to them. Thus, He says to Nathanael, His own newfound disciple, a friend of Philip the Apostle, "'I saw you under the fig-tree before Philip spoke to you'" (John 1.49). *Cat's Eye*

saffron Savior: a common Hermetic symbol—Christ conceived as the Sol Novus, "before whom the lesser stars pale." In effect, being transformational, like the philosophical gold, "He is the affirmation of the daylight of consciousness in trinitarian form" (Jung, *Alchemical Studies* 242). *The Round Dance of the Stars*

The sage, assembled, dries over a stone / His heated heartbeat: The speaker refers to "the motif of torture"—a crucial element in "the phenomenology of the individuation process as the alchemists experienced it" and to one "gruesome" recipe in particular: "the drying of a man over a heated stone" (Jung, *Alchemical Studies* 328-29). Jung notes that, ironically, it is the artifex himself who, having projected himself into the material substance—the "stone"—of the *opus,* "cannot endure the torments" (329). *Light of the Eye*

sail beaming: The speaker refers to advances in light *beaming* technology — specifically, to laser sails—and to the Starshot program that aims to accelerate microchip-size nanocraft at relativistic speeds to Alpha Centauri, the next goal of humankind on its journey to the stars. Thus, in *sail beaming,* "a laser array would propel [numerous] miniature laser sails at a spacecraft, and the impact of these bullets would drive the spacecraft forward." See Charles Q. Choi, "So How Exactly Do We Get to Alpha Centauri?" *Popular Science* 12 Apr. 2016: 5 <www.popsci.com>. *Drilling on Mars*

Salt- or sun-point: "The *point* is most akin to the nature of light, and light [like the *Sun*] is a *simulacrum Dei*" (Jung, *Alchemical Studies* 151). See also Jung, *The Archetypes and the Collective Unconscious* 328, where "Salt, in ecclesiastical as well as alchemical usage, is the symbol [. . .] for the distinguished or elect *personality,*" i.e., an analogue of the God-man, as in Matthew 5.13: "'You are salt to the world.'" *Scout*

sapphirine: a word that evokes the mystical sapphire stone, in alchemy "'the sapphire blue flower of the hermaphrodite,'" the latter enigma being a symbol of the self, i.e., both a psychic totality and "a being that is forever dying yet eternal" (Jung, *Alchemical Studies* 259). See also Jung, *Psychology and Alchemy,* including fig. 30, and Jung, *Mysterium Coniunctionis* 59-60. *Gateway; Light of the Eye*

Saturn fed / On Gaea's biped: The Roman god *Saturn* was one of the Titans, the same as the Greek god Cronus. In this poem, *Gaea's biped*—an imagined *future* version of NASA's Robonaut 2—is a stand-in for Rhea's son, Zeus. See the note on *Some god had spat him* given below. *The Moon in Transition Raised to the Sun*

Schrödinger's Cat: According to the probabilistic nature of the new physics, "the observer in the quantum-mechanical world" not only "manipulates," but also "participates" in every event that he perceives. He may even inhabit separate yet parallel realities. As Harth demonstrates in *Windows on the Mind,* "The situation has been described by a bizarre example known as 'Schrödinger's cat' [after the Austrian physicist Erwin Schrödinger (1887-1961)]. This hapless creature [the equally eerie counterpart of Alice's vanishing Cheshire cat] is locked in a box with a 'hellish contraption' consisting of a small amount of radioactive substance, a Geiger counter, a hammer rigged to be released by the counter, and a glass vial of cyanide placed to be broken by the hammer. The sequence of events is thus:

particle from decay of radioactive substance triggers Geiger counter, Geiger counter trips hammer, hammer smashes vial, cyanide escapes and kills cat." However, "In the absence of an observation, the *complete* quantum-mechanical description of the radioactive substance would be that it has both decayed and *not* decayed, [with] the counter both tripped and not tripped, the hammer both up and down, the vial both smashed and intact, the cat both dead and alive." In short, given the Copenhagen or solipsistic view of quantum mechanics, "Only when [you] take a look is the matter decided one way or the other [. . .]." By contrast, given the many-universes interpretation, "The moment you open the box to check on Schrödinger's cat, there will be two different worlds, one in which you observe a healthy cat jumping out of the box, the other in which *another you* finds the cat poisoned" (223-24). *Schrödinger's Cat*

scintilla's scan: In medieval alchemy, a *scintilla* is a soul-spark that reflects God's descent into matter. Jung describes this phenomenon in *Alchemical Studies:* According to the alchemists, "in the very darkness of nature a light is hidden, a little spark without which the darkness would not be darkness [. . .]. The light from above made the darkness still darker, but the *lumen naturae* [the divine spark buried in the darkness] is the light of darkness itself, which illuminates its own darkness, and this light the darkness comprehends [. . .]." In short, "Not separation of the natures [human as well as divine] but union of the natures was the goal of alchemy" (160-61). See also *Mysterium Coniunctionis* 491, where Jung identifies even further the conduit to such wholeness: "In the unconscious are hidden those 'sparks of light' [*scintillae*], the archetypes, from which a higher meaning can be 'extracted.' The 'magnet' that attracts the hidden thing is the self, or in this case the 'theoria' or the symbol representing it, which the adept uses as an instrument." Here the term *scan* implies either swift, cleansing, sequential, or systematic scrutiny. *Scintilla's Scan*

scion: "a descendant; [an] offspring" ("Scion" [n.], def. 2)—here, of both Christ and Abraham. See Gal. 3.26-29: "For through faith you are all sons of God in union with Christ Jesus. Baptized into union with him, you have all put on Christ as a garment. There is no such thing as Jew and Greek, slave and freeman, male and female; for you are all one person in Christ Jesus. But if you thus belong to Christ, you are the 'issue' of Abraham, and so heirs by promise." *Cat's Eye; Circumambient; Extract of the Macrocosm; The Jesus of Psychoanalysis; A Methane Snow; The Round Dance of the Stars; Scion; Scout; The Water That Does Not Make the Hands Wet; Waxing in Luna into the Nature of the Sun*

the scion in the pleat: the Christian Savior entwined in "Clotho's [competing] skein" and in a cumulous cloud. Here, the *pleat* may also function as "a symbol of involution" (Chevalier and Gheerbrant, *The Penguin Dictionary of Symbols* 759), i.e., psychologically, an infolding, a curling inward, in the holistic evolution of "an 'extra-conscious' psyche whose contents are *personal,* and an 'extra-conscious' psyche whose contents are *impersonal* and *collective*" (Jung, *Aion* 7). *A Methane Snow*

Scion regimented as a crystal: the Spirit of the glorified Jesus—the "*Christ in us*" (Murray, *The Spirit of Christ* 85), His faith-based believer-priests. In his *Homiliae in Ezechielem (Homilies on Ezekiel),* Saint Gregory the Great [c. 540-604] explains that, through the "glory" of His resurrection, Christ "hardened after the fashion of a crystal from water, so that there was one and the same nature in it and in [H]im [. . .]" (qtd. in Jung,

Mysterium Coniunctionis 449n345), like "heavenly light" (Chevalier and Gheerbrant, *The Penguin Dictionary of Symbols* 267). *Scion*

scree: a pile of loose stones or rocky detritus lying at the foot of a hill or at the base of a cliff. *Schrödinger's Cat*

seahorse that floats amid frond or fan: In this passage, the speaker who "sought to be neither woman nor man, / But both these sexes" (lines 4-5) refers, without irony, to the amazing pregnancy of the male *seahorse*. Thus, after the female fish "lays her eggs in an armored chamber (marsupium) of his belly, the sperm-producing male "fertilizes the eggs"; broods them "for about four weeks, while they are nourished by secretions from the spongy wall of his brood pouch"; and then, "over a period of 24 hours, [. . .] undergoes a series of shuddering contractions," even as "the perfectly formed young seahorses are expelled in large numbers" (Jane Reynolds, Phil Gates, and Gaden Robinson, *365 Days of Nature and Discovery* [New York: Abrams, 1994] 108). *Rebis*

a sea of pearl: here, "the waters of the psyche," since "Water is the commonest symbol for the unconscious" (Jung, *The Archetypes and the Collective Unconscious* 18). For psychological reasons, the color of the *sea* is blue *pearl*—or sapphire blue with a nautical undertone—not only because "the unconscious in man has feminine characteristics" (Jung, *Psychology and Alchemy* 214), but also because "the 'golden flower of alchemy' [. . .] can sometimes be a blue flower: 'The sapphire blue flower of the hermaphrodite'" (80). *Mastermind*

Secret sulphur: According to the alchemists, *sulphur* is not only a synonym for the "arcane substance" (Jung, *Alchemical Studies* 74), but also "'the fire hidden in Mercurius,'" the two-sided avatar of the masculine principle in its diabolical aspect (228n32). *Light of the Eye*

seas from Ymir's (EE-meerz) sweat: in Old Norse cosmology, the slain primeval giant from whose flesh the earth was created and from whose *sweat* the sea. *Fabricator*

Selene: the ancient Greek moon-goddess. Her lover was Endymion, the androgynous shepherd. *The Woman in the Moon*

Self-heated, we incubate: See Jung, *Mysterium Coniunctionis* 203-04, where the "chariot of Aristotle"—a symbol of the self—is "immersed in the sea of the unconscious for the purpose of heating and incubation, corresponding to the state of *tapas* [TUH-pus], incubation by means of 'self-heating.' By this is obviously meant a state of introversion in which the unconscious content is brooded over and digested" until—having developed [like an embryo] and taken form ["Incubate" [vi.], def. 2]—"it is recognized and made an object of conscious discrimination." *The Chariot of Aristotle's Wheels*

SenSuit: See Dan O'Shea, "SenSuit helps humans control robot co-workers," *Fierce Electronics* 19 July 2021: 1-2 <www.fierceelectronics.com>: "The Guardian XT robot, which itself is the top half of the Sarcos Guardian XO robotic exoskeleton, is expected to be available by the end of next year. It will integrate Sarcos' SenSuit wearer controller and a high definition, virtual reality or augmented reality-based head-mounted display, providing situational awareness and enabling workers to have intuitive control of the robot. The robot will be equipped with three degrees of freedom and will be able to use the same common trade tools [that] humans use." See also Menzel and D'Aluisio, *Robo sapiens* 130: "'when someone wears the telepresence gear[,] what we try to convey to the person is that they become the robot.'" *The Cusp of Skill*

Seraphim: the plural form of *seraph;* "any of the highest order of angels, above the cherubim" ("Seraphim" [n.], def. 2). *The Round Dance of the Stars*

A sevenfold star: In alchemical texts, Mercurius is the *sevenfold star* that appears "at the end of the work" (Jung, *Mysterium Coniunctionis* 225n8). In this poem, as "the analogue of Christ" (235), the NASA astronaut, like Mercurius, also "heralds," as Venus, the morning star, does, "only much more directly, the coming of the light" (226). *The Heavenly Journey of the Shaman*

Shaman: either a priest or a magus or a holy man with supernatural powers. *Christ on Einstein's Tram; Containment and the Cosmic Edge; The Heavenly Journey of the Shaman; Light of the Eye; Schrödinger's Cat*

shard: "a fragment or broken piece, esp. of pottery" ("Shard" [n.], def. 1). *Scion*

Shells of infrared: various dust shells ejected "at intervals of 500 to 1,700 years" by CW Leonis, a carbon-rich red giant star "no longer visible to the naked eye," since "the light emitted from the star is infrared. [. . .] In five billion years, our own sun will also swell into a red giant star. When it cools, it will produce large quantities of dust in the outermost layers of its atmosphere" [shells that a space telescope equipped with PACS (the Photodetector Array Camera and Spectrometer) can capture]. Thus, "Observing and understanding the episodes in the history of CW Leonis will help astronomers determine the fate of the sun." See Leuven University, "Giant star expels multiple dust shells," *Phys.org* 28 Sept. 2011: 1-4 <www.phys.org>. *Cosmic Dust*

Shem: In Gen. 5.32, *Shem* is one of the sons of Noah; in Luke 3.36, Jesus is a descendant of *Shem*. See also the notes on *Shem's enigma* and *Shem's second birth* given below. *Chain-Linked*

Shem's enigma: the manikin that learns: i.e., either NASA's Robonaut or Alchemy's metallic homunculus (Jung, *Alchemical Studies* 89), here a surprising, even baffling prefiguration of the Old Testament "good stewards" who—as spiritual descendants of Shem, the eldest son of Noah—shall dispense "the grace of God in its various forms" until the Rapture (1 Pet. 4.10). *Fabricator*

Shem's second birth: / His tabernacled Son: In the "mythologized ethnology" of Genesis, Shem is both the eldest son of Noah and the "eponymous" ancestor "of the Hebrews and their various cognates" (Bernard E. Lewis, "Who Are the Semites?" *My Jewish Learning* [n.d.]: 1 <www.myjewishlearning.com>. Accessed 28 Sept. 2020.) In Psalm 45.7, the prophet Shem is also an "anointed" precursor of the Messiah. See the note on *His tabernacled Son* given above. *Circumambient*

Shepherd of Aries: Christ characterized as both shepherd and Paschal lamb, in astrology a symbol "coinciding with the expiring aeon of Aries" [the Ram] and with "the great conjunction" [of Jupiter and Saturn] in Pisces, the House of the Fishes, the sign of the coming Messiah (Jung, *Aion* 103). *Christ on Einstein's Tram*

Shriven substance: either an offspring of both Christ and Abraham (Gal. 3.26-29) or the Christian speaker himself heard and absolved by confessing ("Shrive" [vt.], 1, 2). *Christ on Einstein's Tram*

sidewise Adam: i.e., "turned or moving toward or from one side" ("Sidewise" [adj.], def.). See Jung, *Mysterium Coniunctionis* 408: In a relevant passage, Jung indicates that, at the Creation, the true hermaphroditic Adam "must have had two faces, in accordance with [the Rabbinic] interpretation of Psalm 139.5: 'Thou hast beset me behind and before' [. . .]." *The Round Dance of the Stars*

sieve: a sifter, a symbol "of the separation of good from evil, of the righteous from the wicked" (Chevalier and Gheerbrant, *The Penguin Dictionary of Symbols* 881). See Luke 22.31-32: "'Simon, Simon, take heed: Satan has been given leave to sift all of you like wheat; but for you I have prayed that your faith may not fail; and when you have come to yourself, you must lend strength to your brothers.'" *Light of the Eye*

sigil: either "a seal" or "an image or [a] sign supposedly having some mysterious power in magic or astrology" ("Sigil" [n.], defs. 1, 2). *Christ on Einstein's Tram; Ephesian Symbols*

Sikh (SEEK): "a member of a Hindu religious sect founded in northern India about 1500 and based on belief in one God and on rejection of the caste system and of idolatry" ("Sikh" [n.], def.). *Fabricator*

silence in the ear / Evokes the light the nearer that we peer: The speaker refers to one of the greatest achievements "in 500 years of modern astronomy." In 1965 Arno Penzias and Robert Wilson detected "the radiation left over from the fireball that filled the Universe at the beginning of its existence." Quite by accident, they made their discovery with a large horn antenna "built like an oversized ear trumpet [. . .] sensitive to faint radio whispers that travel through the Universe" (Robert Jastrow, *God and the Astronomers* [New York: Norton, 1978] 20-21). *Fabricator*

silicone: i.e., rubber *silicone*, the material used to construct tactile robotic skin. *Circumambient; The Cusp of Skill; Ephesian Symbols*

Silver in Cabeus, plume in the sky: On October 9, 2009, the "twin impacts" of NASA's Lunar Crater Observation and Sensing Satellite [LCROSS] and its spent Centaur upper stage rocket in the moon's Cabeus [kuh-BAY-us] crater "lifted a plume [a mass or stream] of material that might not have seen direct sunlight for billions of years." After the impacts, "grains of mostly pure water ice [from the débris *plume*] were lofted into the sunlight in the vacuum of space," indicating that "the moon is chemically active and has a water cycle." In fact, beside the water molecules, NASA's suite of instruments "discovered large amounts of light metals such as sodium, mercury, and possibly even silver" (Rachel Hoover, Nancy Neal Jones, and Michael Braukus, "NASA Missions Uncover the Moon's Buried Treasures," *NASA* 21 Oct. 2010: 1-2 <www.nasa.gov>). *Light of the Eye*

silver in the spear: a classical play of opposites. See Chevalier and Gheerbrant, *The Penguin Dictionary of Symbols:* "The spear is universally regarded as an axial, phallic, fiery or solar" symbol (900), while "silver is the passive, female, lunar, watery, and cold principle" (882). *Fabricator*

Since all Creation wears Her feather-dress: See *The Penguin Dictionary of Symbols* 373, where Chevalier and Gheerbrant remind us that "the symbolic function of feathers is linked with the ritual of ascent into Heaven and hence with second sight and divination." *The Woman in the Moon*

skein: "a quantity of thread or yarn wound in a coil' ("Skein" [n.], def. 1a)—here, the trajectory of Robonaut, NASA's "state-of-the-art humanoid" designed for space travel (Menzel and D'Aluisio, *Robo sapiens* 129). In this passage, the Spinner is Clotho, in Greek myth one of three sororal Fates. *Evangelist*

Skein encased in a shell of water ice, / Jupiter's Europa: One of Jupiter's four largest Galilean moons, including Io, Ganymede, and Callisto, *Europa* "is covered with an extremely smooth shell of water ice. There is probably an ocean of liquid water below the shell, warmed by the same forces that heat Io's volcanoes" (Amanda Barnett, "Basics of Spaceflight: Solar System Exploration," *NASA Science* n.d.: 11-12 <https://solarsystem.nasa.gov>. Accessed 10 January 2022. *A Host-Star in Draco*

slope rock or scree: See Paul D. Spudis, "Slopes, Streaks and Flows," *Air & Space Magazine* (17 Nov. 2011: 1 <https: "Mass wasting [on the Moon] includes both gradual, infinitesimally slow soil creep on slopes and rapid, catastrophic mass movements, called landslides. Long trains of rock debris can form *scree* slopes, loose fragments lying precariously at the critical angle beyond which they move, the *angle of repose*. Because impact craters make steep walls and the larger ones bring up peaks in their centers, most mass wasting on the Moon is found in and around impact craters of all sizes." *Schrödinger's Cat*

smoke-hole of the tent: In *The Penguin Dictionary of Symbols,* Chevalier and Gheerbrant describe an entrance that is "an invitation to a voyage into the beyond." Thus, "the transit from Earth to Heaven is made through 'the gateway of the sun,' which symbolizes release from the cosmos beyond the constraints of the human condition. This [opening] is the eye of the dome or the smoke-hole of the tent through which passes the World Axis. It is also the crown of the head and most of all the 'strait' gate which leads to the Kingdom of Heaven, notionally expressed by the rope or camel passing through the eye of a needle" (422). See the note on *Eye of the dome* given above. *The Smoke-Hole of the Tent*

snow: a symbol of the *albedo,* one of the main goals in the alchemical process. "It is the silver or moon condition," a purified state "which still has to be raised to the sun condition. The *albedo* is, so to speak, the daybreak, but not till the *rubedo* is it sunrise" (Jung, *Psychology and Alchemy* 232). See also Jung, *Alchemical Studies* 214, where the mercurial life-force "flies like solid white snow." *Gatekeeper*

Sol: here, "the rising sun—the *Sol mysticus,*" i.e., the pre-existent Christ: "the reborn as his own begetter" (Jung, *Symbols of Transformation* 322-23). *Gatekeeper*

Sol's entelechy; immanent His plan, / The New Jerusalem in the inner man: In *Mysterium Coniunctionis,* Jung writes that, in medieval alchemy, the numinous figure of Mercurius often mirrors the divine syzygy of Sol and Luna, symbols that underscore "the duality of our psychic life." In fact, "the concept of Sol has not a little to do with the growth of modern consciousness" as an offshoot of God's temporal or earthly involvement with humankind. In effect, *Sol's entelechy* is actualized essence—the immortal Self: "the heavenly Jerusalem in the inner man." However, according to Jung, the "necessary counterpart" of consciousness is "a dark, latent, non-manifest side, the unconscious, whose [shaded] presence can be known [paradoxically] only by the [searing] light of consciousness" (96-97). See also the note on *Some sapphirine premise* given below, and the equally pertinent passage from Rev. 22.14, where assemblies of Spirit-filled believers—"those who wash their robes clean"—gather in "the holy city, new Jerusalem" (21.2) at End-time. *Mastermind*

Some epiphenomenon of the brain: In this poem, "Gaea's swain"—Spacetime's prefigured "lover or suitor" ("Swain" [n.], def. 3)—is either Christ or else the Christ-man, the speaker himself, the collateral entity that occurs with and seems to result from certain neural processes in the brain but that cannot explain its source, the elusive noumenon: the postulated ground of each actualized essence. In other words, in Kantian philosophy, the phenomenon —the thing as it appears in perception—is markedly different from the noumenon, "the thing as it is in itself," the latter object being independent of sense experience and otherwise unknowable. *Evangelist*

Some god had spat him: The speaker evokes a well-known, cosmogonic Greek myth. Thus, when "Cronus, the lord of the universe, had learned that one of his children was destined some day to dethrone him, he rebelled against his fate by swallowing them as soon as they were born." However, "when Rhea bore Zeus, her sixth child, she succeeded in having him secretly carried off to Crete, while she gave her husband a great stone wrapped in swaddling clothes which he supposed was the baby and swallowed down accordingly." Nevertheless, later, "when Zeus was grown, he forced his father with the help of his grandmother, the Earth, to disgorge" the anointed stone "along with the five earlier children" (Hamilton, *Mythology* 65-66). *Containment and the Cosmic Edge*

some numinous tract / In tunnels of the moon that Gaea stacked, / The *rebis* scrolled, and the hierophant cracked: / Astral symbolon, autonomous fact: Like the *rebis,* "an amalgam of Sol and Luna," (Jung, *Psychology and Alchemy* 202), Christ is both an "[Astral] symbolon" (183), i.e., "an outward image as [universal] creed" (14), and "an autonomous psychological fact" (185). The "imprinted archetype" (14) of the Savior is also either a figure in "an ancient book in the form of a rolled manuscript" ("Scroll" [n.], def. 2), or a secret code "solved" ("Crack[1]" [vt.], def. 7), or the alternate subject of this *tract* or treatise ("Tract[2]" [n.], def. 1): the starry pioneer in outer space. *The Man in the Moon*

Some sapphirine premise: the heaven-sent conviction that "The [eternal] Word is Spirit-breathed" (Murray, *The Spirit of Christ* 228). Murray explains that "In the creation of the world, it was the work of the Spirit to put Himself into contact with the dark and lifeless matter of chaos, and by His quickening energy to give it the power of life and fruitfulness. It was only after it had been vitalized by Him that the Word of God gave it form and called forth all the different types of life and beauty we now see. In the creation of man, it was also the Spirit that was breathed into the body that had been formed from the ground. The Spirit united itself with what would otherwise be dead matter" (166). *Courtship*

Sometimes a missile darts across the skies— / Spear of Archytas: See the note on *Spears that vanish* given below. *The Spear of Archytas*

So, Typhon pursuing him, Pisces shunts / In the wettest place that the foetus fronts: In Greek mythology, *Typhon,* the monster with a hundred heads, had pursued Leto when her son Apollo "was still in her womb; but she fled to the floating island of Delos on a 'night sea journey' and was there safely delivered of her child" (Jung, *Symbols of Transformation* 371). Here, of course, *Pisces,* who *shunts* or turns aside in order to conquer the serpent, represents not only Christ, both sun-hero and "Goat-Fish," but also His womb-entwining coheir, the speaker himself. In other words, the latterday galactic pilgrim, being reborn, has just emerged—like the Son of God—from "'the wettest place on earth,' [. . .] the maternal depths" (198). *Rebis*

soul-spark: in Cabalistic texts, the spirit that descends into matter. See the note on *Spark in the semen* given below. *Circumambient; A Methane Snow; Trapeze*

A sower, His seed, and rivers that flow: See Matthew 13.36-39: "his disciples came to him and said, 'Explain to us the parable of the darnel [the weedy, even toxic rye grass] in the field.' And this was his answer: 'The sower of the good seed is the Son of Man. The field is the world; the good seed stands for the children of the Kingdom, the darnel for the children of the evil one. The enemy who sowed the darnel is the devil. The harvest is the end of time,'" when "'the righteous will shine as brightly as the sun in the kingdom of their Father.'" Significantly, in this line from the poem, the speaker refers not only to the "Streams of living water [that] shall flow out from within him" (John 7.38), i.e., from the Spirit of the glorified Christ, but also to the four rivers of Paradise, "the abode of the originally androgynous Primordial Man (Adam)" (Jung, *Aion* 210). *The Smoke-Hole of the Tent*

Sown from antinomies: The Christian pilgrim confronts the irreconcilable opposites—the increasing "tension between above and below"—in "the progressive development and differentiation of consciousness." Thus, "The psychological concept of the self, in part derived from our knowledge of the whole man, but for the rest depicting itself spontaneously in the products of the unconscious as an archetypal quaternity bound together by inner antinomies, cannot omit the shadow that belongs to the light figure, for without it this figure lacks body and humanity." Simply enough, "In the empirical self, light and shadow form a paradoxical unity" (Jung, *Aion* 42-44). *Psalter*

Sown from the ash, the mother of lances: In various cultures, a masculine significance attaches to both the lance and the *ash*. Thus, according to the ancient Greeks, "Ash was the wood used for spear-shafts and a metaphor for the weapon itself" (Chevalier and Gheerbrant, *The Penguin Dictionary of Symbols* 50). Furthermore, because "the ash is the mother of lances," men of the Bronze Age "are descended from her" (Jung, *Symbols of Transformation* 288). In fact, in the legend of Kaineus [KEYE-noose], the hero "commanded that his lance was to be worshipped," probably because "he thinks [that] it is a valid equivalent of himself." Interestingly, "Pindar says of this Kaineus that [. . .] he descended into the depths, splitting the earth with a straight foot," an action that Jung interprets as nothing less than the hero's claim to rebirth, and hence to immortality, "through entry into the mother." As if to italicize "the typical elements of a [bisexual] libido myth," Jung adds that, originally, Kaineus "is supposed to have been a maiden named Kainis [KEYE-nis], who, as a reward for her [sexual] submissiveness, was changed by Poseidon into an invulnerable man" (288-89). *Splitting the Earth with a Straight Foot*

Spacetime fostered, Singularity pearled: The speaker refers not only to the débris that erupted from a big bang singularity [the point of infinite compression at which space and time cease to exist] and that "was literally the creation of the universe" (Davies, *Other Worlds* 102), but also to Kafka's concept of "pearling" and "to the singular sounds [. . .] of a certain 'nothing' searching its name," in "Josephine the Singer, or the Mouse Folk," a "longer story" written in 1924. Samuel Weber explores an "aporetical" or irresolvable reading of Kafka's text throughout Chapter 18 of *Singularity: Politics and Poetics* (Minnesota / London: U of Minnesota P, 2021). *Light of the Eye*

Spacetime's Leviathan: in the Bible, "a sea monster," either reptile or whale ("Leviathan" [n.], def. 1). In alchemy, *Leviathan* becomes, like the raven, a symbol of the transforming substance. See Jung, *Psychology and Alchemy* 134, 464. *The Path of Least Action*

spagyric: The word *spagyric* refers to an alchemical process that both separates and combines (Jung, *Mysterium Coniunctionis* 481n91). Thus, the *spagyric foetus* ascends into Heaven that it may become a spirit from a body and then descends to earth that it may become a body again. Elsewhere, Jung explains that "The spagyric birth (*spagyrica foetura*) is nothing other than the *filius philosophorum,* the inner, eternal man in the shell of the outer, mortal man" (*Alchemical Studies* 150). Cf. John 3.13: "No one ever went up into heaven except the one who came down from heaven, the Son of Man whose home is in heaven."

Cat's Eye; Containment and the Cosmic Edge; Courtship; Evangelist; The Heavenly Journey of the Shaman; Mastermind; The Smoke-Hole of the Tent; Storyboard

The spagyric foetus spun in His womb: In "the ancient Greek view Hermes [as the Spirit of Mercurius] was a wind-god" (Jung, *Psychology and Alchemy* 387). Accordingly, in the text of the *Emerald Tablet,* the *spagyric foetus* is "the renewed Mercurius" [a synonym for the Holy Ghost] that dwells in "the alchemical Mercurius in his aerial aspect" because "The wind hath carried it in his belly" (387, fig. 210). *Mastermind*

spagyric gum: *gum* arabic, or "blessed" red *gum,* not only the "'resin of the wise'—a synonym for the transforming substance"—but also "the [alchemical] medium between mind and body and the union of both" (Jung, *Psychology and Alchemy* 161, 401). In *Mysterium Coniunctionis* 481n91, Jung offers helpful root definitions of the word *spagyric:* either "to rend, tear, [or] stretch out" or "to bring or collect together." *Local Bubble*

spar: here, "any pole, as a mast, yard, boom, or gaff, supporting or extending a sail of a ship" ("Spar" [n.] def. 1). *Schrödinger's Cat*

Spark in the semen: i.e., a soul-*spark*—the spirit that descends into matter. See Jung, *Mysterium Coniunctionis,* where "Heraclitus, 'the [Greek] physicist' [fl. about 500 BC], is said to have conceived the soul as 'a spark of stellar essence'" (48) and, even more pertinently, where "Simon Magus [Acts 8.9-13] teaches that in semen and milk there is a very small spark which 'increases and becomes a power boundless and immutable'" (49). *Fabricator*

The Spear of Archytas: See the note on *Spears that vanish* given below. *The Spear of Archytas*

Spears that vanish: The speaker refers to "the cosmic-edge riddle—'what happens to a spear when it is hurled across the outer boundary of the universe'—that was posed by Archytas of Tarentum [c. 428 BC–c. 350 BC], a Pythagorean soldier-philosopher and friend of Plato. [. . .] 'Does the spear rebound or vanish from the world?' he asked. The riddle exposed the logical inconsistency of believing that whatever bounds the universe is itself not part of the universe." Because the universe contains everything, there is no outside. In other words, "the riddle of Archytas abolished the cosmic edge" (Harrison: *Cosmology: The Science of the Universe* 149-50). Elsewhere, Carl Huffman, illustrating the subject even as he defends the same thesis, "asks anyone who argues that the universe is limited [rather than unlimited] to engage in a thought experiment [. . .]: 'If I arrived at the outermost edge of the heavens, could I extend my hand or staff into what is outside or not? It would be paradoxical [given our normal assumptions about the nature of space] not to be able to extend it.'" In effect, "The end of the staff, once extended[,] will mark a new limit. Archytas can advance to the new limit and ask the same question again, so that there will always be something, into which his staff [or, as in this poem, his spear] can be extended, beyond the supposed limit, and hence that something is clearly unlimited" ("Archytas," *Stanford Encyclopedia of Philosophy* 23 Aug. 2016: 19 <plato.stanford.edu>). *Containment and the Cosmic Edge*

The spherical tomb of Hermes that heals: In medieval alchemy, the artifex "called his vessel a [spherical] tomb" (Jung, *Mysterium Coniunctionis* 64), a sepulcher from which the mythical philosophers' stone—i.e., "the [projected] inner Christ, [the] God in man" (Jung, *Alchemical Studies* 96)—was to be removed. *The Chariot of Aristotle's Wheels*

spheroid: here, an oblate *spheroid*—like the Sun, the Moon, and the Earth, "a body that is almost but not quite a sphere" ("Spheroid" [n.], def.). *Claim; The Man in the Moon; Storyboard*

The Spindle Galaxy: Discovered by Pierre Méchain in 1781, the *Spindle Galaxy*, also known as M102, "is located 44 million light-years from Earth in the constellation Draco." Incredibly, its "outer halo is dotted with numerous globular cluster stars, gravitationally bound clusters of nearly a million stars each. Background galaxies that are millions to billions of light-years farther away than M102 are also seen through its halo." Rob Garner describes these phenomena in "Messier 102 (The Spindle Galaxy)," *Hubble's Messier Catalog* 19 Oct. 2017:1-4 <www.nasa.gov/feature/goddard/2017/messier-102-the-spindle-galaxy>. *Cat's Eye*

the Spinner: In Greek mythology, Clotho, one of three Fates, spins the thread of life that Lachesis measures and that Atropos cuts. *The Smoke-Hole of the Tent*

a starker rite / Than the node at new moon: The speaker evokes the "strange, eerie specter" of a solar eclipse. See Engelbrektson, *Stars, Planets, and Galaxies* 67: "At an angle of about 5°, the moon crosses the ecliptic twice each month at two points called nodes. When the sun is at or near a node at new moon, an eclipse of the sun can occur"—a bleak and "frightening experience." Of course, here, the "starker rite" is the darkness of the grave. *Spacetime's Wight*

stave by stave: The speaker refers to "the thin, shaped strips of wood or metal, set edge to edge to form or strengthen the wall of a [. . .] bucket" ("Stave" [n.], def. 1). The definition of *staves* given below is also pertinent. *The Jesus of Psychoanalysis*

staves: sets "of verses, or lines, of a song or poem; stanza[s]" ("Stave" [n.], def. 3). *Storyboard*

Still galaxies slide or mix in the light, [. . .] / Courtship in the cosmos the strangest rite: Cf. Begley, "When Galaxies Collide" 5: "Galaxies close enough together to feel each other's gravity undergo a coy, slow courtship. When they meet, they might slide by, passing in the night like cosmic strangers. But they might, instead, collide. Our own Milky Way is now swallowing a dwarf galaxy called Sagittarius." *Courtship*

Still the world is edgeless—without a bight: According to current scientific data, the shape of the universe has neither edge nor curve. In fact, overall, on a large scale—as Nola Taylor Redd reports—it is *flat*. See "What is the shape of the universe?" *Space.com* 15 Jan. 2014: 3 <www.space.com>. In this context, the term *bight* refers to the "circular segment of a curve" (<www.vocabulary.com/dictionary/bight>). *Containment and the Cosmic Edge*

stone: in alchemy, the mysterious *lapis philosophorum,* the philosophers' *stone,* a symbolic "parallel of Christ" (Jung, *Alchemical Studies* 96, 320). See also 1 Pet. 2.5: "Come, and let yourselves be built, as living stones, into a spiritual temple; become a holy priesthood, to offer spiritual sacrifices acceptable to God through Jesus Christ." The notes on *Stone that incubates* and *the stone that is no stone,* given below, are doubly clarifying. *Christ on Einstein's Tram; Ephesian Symbols; Fabricator; Here Be Dragons; Mastermind; Scion*

stone that, heated, dries: The speaker refers to "the motif of torture"—a crucial element in "the phenomenology of the individuation process as the alchemists experienced it"—and to one "gruesome" recipe in particular: "the drying of a man over a heated stone" (Jung, *Alchemical Studies* 328-29). Jung notes that, ironically, it is the artifex himself who, having projected himself into the material substance—the "stone"—of the *opus,* "cannot endure the torments" (329). *The Spear of Archytas*

Stone that incubates: The speaker refers to the transformational *lapis*—in effect, *the stone that has a spirit:* "the figure of light veiled in matter" (Jung, *Alchemical Studies* 247). See also *Alchemical Studies* 292n3, where the earthly stone (the *filius microcosmi*) "'is an outstanding type and lifelike image of the incarnation of Christ.'" Equally pertinent is 1 Thess. 5.5-6: "You are all children of light, children of day. We do not belong to night or darkness [. . .]." *Ephesian Symbols*

the stone that is no stone: in alchemy, the philosophers' stone taken as a symbol of the unified self, i.e., "of the inner Christ, of God in man" (Jung, *Alchemical Studies* 96, 291n9). See also the note on *Stone that incubates* given above. *Fabricator; Mastermind*

strapped to the wall / Even as a bean, a plant, or a ball: These lines echo Sheila Kitzinger's succinct description of the unfolding natal journey: "When the ball [of cells] reached the uterus it began to grow roots, like the roots of a plant [. . .] that didn't look much like a baby yet—more like a sprouting bean" (*Being Born* 19, 22). *The Heavenly Journey of the Shaman*

Stumbling Stone: The speaker refers to Christ—for believers, the Rock that saves (1 Cor. 10.4) and, for unbelievers, the Stone "against and over which they shall stumble" (Isa. 8.14). *Cat's Eye*

Substance he bleeds— / [. . .] Light's metabolized screeds, / Ashen extracts: The speaker alludes, figuratively, to the product of alchemy's "redeeming *opus*" (Jung, *Psychology and Alchemy* 306)—here, sublimated souls obtained as living Power Books of God. *Here Be Dragons*

Substance hypostatized: The speaker underscores a key Christian doctrine: "the [hypostatic] union of the wholly divine nature and of a wholly human nature in the one person of Jesus Christ" ("Hypostasis" [n.], def. 4c). *Schrödinger's Cat*

The substance of the stone: the weightless key—"the regenerated earth [construed] as a stone lacking all weight" because "it is evident that nothing material, which alone has weight, is left over, and all that remains is the psychic content of the projection" (Jung, *Mysterium Coniunctionis* 204). See also the note on *Stone that incubates* and on *the stone that is no stone* given above. *The Chariot of Aristotle's Wheels*

such twine as ravels in the street: i.e., in a cloud *street,* a row of lumpy, dynamic cumulus clouds oriented almost parallel to the direction of the wind. The image also evokes the myth of Theseus, the Greek hero who plies Ariadne's ball of *twine* even as he pursues the bull-headed Minotaur in the labyrinth of darkness that, almost perversely, "takes one to the centre of oneself" (Chevalier and Gheerbrant, *The Penguin Dictionary of Symbols* 644). *A Methane Snow*

Sulfates in the chasma: According to Alfred McEwen, a University of Arizona geologist, Melas Chasma [a canyon on Mars], despite "all its geologic riches, [. . .] lacks any obvious reservoir to keep a crew alive and provide fuel for their return rocket home. McEwen's solution is to squeeze water from stones," moisture that must have "become locked into minerals in the rocks." In fact, "Images from HiRISE [NASA's High-Resolution Imaging Science Experiment] and other instruments suggest that Melas Chasma is rich in polyhydrated sulfates, minerals that by volume are up to half water." See Lee Billings, "No Man's Land: Where on Mars Should Astronauts Go?" *Scientific American* 4 Mar. 2016: 11 <www.scientificamerican.com>. *Fixated on Mars*

Sulphur: in alchemystical texts, a synonym for "the arcane [or transformative] substance" (Jung, *Alchemical Studies* 74). Thus, "The hermaphroditic Venus was regarded as typifying the coniunctio of Sulphur and Mercurius" (187n26), the latter figure being both the "healer [or preserver] of all imperfect bodies" and "the analogue of Christ" (235). *Ephesian Symbols; Fabricator; Light of the Eye; The Water That Does Not Make the Hands Wet; Waxing in Luna into the Nature of the Sun*

Sulphur in the middle: i.e., in the Earth's mantle, "the vast middle layer between the core and the crust." See The European Association of Geochemistry, "Earth's core contains 90 percent of Earth's sulfur, new research shows," *Science News* 16 June 2017: 2-3 <www.sciencedaily.com>, where the writer reports that, recently, for the first time, scientists "have conclusive geochemical evidence" that sulphur is contained in the Earth's core. Thus, in the "distant" past, "when Earth collided with a large, planet-sized body" and tore off "the part that became our moon," the "cataclysmic" event "left a fingerprint" that "has been used to confirm the core content." In effect, "the impact of the collision melted [the] Earth's mantle, allowing a sulphur-rich liquid to form in the mantle [. . .]." Thereafter, some of the liquid "remained and [sank] into the core." *Fabricator*

Superposition the state that we flee: according to Paul Davies, "a hybrid of two overlapping realities [. . .]. But the inherent uncertainty of quantum mechanics forbids you to know which of these two possibilities will actually prevail" (*The Mind of God* 216). *Schrödinger's Cat*

The surge of planets: Recently, Doug Hudgins, a Kepler program scientist at NASA Headquarters in Washington, noted that, prior to the Kepler Exoplanet Mission, "we knew of perhaps 500 exoplanets across the whole sky. [. . .] Now, in just two years staring at a patch of sky not much bigger than your fist," the Kepler Space Telescope "has discovered more than 60 planets and more than 2,300 planet candidates. This tells us that our galaxy is positively loaded with planets of all sizes and orbits." See "NASA's Kepler announces 11 new planetary systems," 3 Nov. 2020: 2 <www.exoplanets.nasa.gov>. *A Host-Star in Draco*

swain: "a lover or suitor" ("Swain" [n.], def. 3). *Here Be Dragons*

sweat: In alchemy, the arcane substance—the living stone—and its bloody *sweat* are what the *opus* is all about. However, the soul of the stone "must be entirely man [. . .]. He cannot be Christ, for Christ by his blood has already redeemed the world from the consequences of the Fall." Rather, this "'most pure' or 'most true' man" shall "bring about what the sacrificial death of Christ has obviously left unfinished, namely the deliverance of the world from evil." Nevertheless, "like Christ he will sweat a redeeming blood—not natural or ordinary blood, but symbolic blood, a psychic substance, the manifestation of a certain kind of Eros which unites the individual as well as the multitude [. . .] and makes them whole [. . .]" (Jung, *Alchemical Studies* 295-96). In other words, for the alchemist, the "redeeming" bloody *sweat* of the stone is neither more nor less than the "reanimating" heavenly dew (103). (See also Jung, *Mysterium Coniunctionis* 40n229.) *Bootstrap; Cat's Eye; Fabricator*

symbolon: According to Jung, "in the dogmatic and religious model of the life of Christ," the emphasis "has always fallen on the historicity of the Saviour's life, and because of this its symbolical nature has remained in the dark," even though "the Incarnation formed a very essential part of the *symbolon* (creed). The efficacy of dogma, however, by no means rests on Christ's unique historical reality but on its own symbolic nature, by virtue of which it expresses a more or less ubiquitous psychological assumption quite independent of the existence of any dogma. There is thus a 'pre-Christian' as well as a 'non-Christian' Christ, in so far as he is an autonomous psychological fact" (*Psychology and Alchemy* 185). *The Man in the Moon*

Syzygies (SIZ-uh-jeez): paired opposites that represent wholeness—here, Adam/Eve; male/female; Sun/Moon. *Evangelist*

the Tadpole: This spiral galaxy, "which resides about 420 million light-years away in the constellation Draco," is "unlike the textbook images of stately galaxies." Apparently its "distorted shape was caused by a small interloper, a very blue, compact galaxy," whereupon powerful gravitational forces "created the long tail of debris, consisting of stars and gas that stretch out more than 280,000 light-years," a "hit-and-run" by-product of "the galaxy collision. Not insignificantly, the color of these clusters is blue "because they contain very massive stars, which are 10 times hotter and 1 million times brighter than our sun." However, once formed, "the star clusters become redder with age as the most massive and bluest stars exhaust their fuel and burn out." Nevertheless, "These clusters will eventually become old globular clusters similar to those found in essentially all halos of galaxies, including our own Milky Way." In fact, "Two prominent clumps of young bright blue stars in the long tail [that] are separated by a 'gap'—a section that is fainter than the rest of the tail—[. . .] will likely become dwarf galaxies that orbit in the Tadpole's halo." See H. Ford et al., "Hubble nets a cosmic tadpole," *Astronomy* 30 April 2002: 2 <https.://hubblesite.org>. *Cat's Eye*

Tall as a dactyl, tiny as a thumb: a "characteristic disparity" in the portrayal of the diminutive dactyls as being both great and small, like the Cosmic Man, "since the giant Hercules was said to be an Idaean dactyl" in the Upanishads [sacred Hindu texts] and in [Goethe's] *Faust* (Jung, *Symbols of Transformation* 126-27). For another definition and a further clarification of this "ancient" paradox, see the note on *dactyls* given above. *Cat's Eye; A Methane Snow*

tamarind: in tropical Africa, both the sacred tree that symbolizes multiplicity and renewal and the medicinal pulp of its tangy fruit. *A Host-Star in Draco*

tars: a colloquial word for sailors ["Tar^2" (n.), def.]—here, surrogates for the "Translocated," or redeployed, NASA astronauts. *Splitting the Earth with a Straight Foot*

temenos (TEH-meh-NAHS): in Greek mythology, a sacred place, "a taboo area" where one can "meet the unconscious" (Jung, *Psychology and Alchemy* 54). *Circumambient; Psalter; Storyboard*

terebinths: In the Bible, the terebinth is a sacred tree. See Gen. 13.18: "So Abram moved his tent and settled by the terebinths of Mamre at Hebron; and there he built an altar to the Lord." See also the note on *Palm-trees* given above. *Bootstrap; Chain-Linked*

tesseract: a four-dimensional hypercube "that has been unraveled," or unfolded, as a series of "ordinary three-dimensional cubes [. . .] arranged in a three-dimensional cross"—in these poems, a symbol as well as a manifestation of our own "harrowing," unknown, "reassembled," and "seemingly impossible" universe. See Kaku, *Hyperspace* 70, 77-78, and also 72, fig. 3.7: Salvador Dali's 1954 oil-on-canvas painting *Crucifixion (Corpus Hypercubus)*, where the artist depicts Christ "as being crucified on a [crosslike] tesseract." *Bootstrap; Christ on Einstein's Tram; Cosmic Dust*

tesseract purled: The speaker refers to "an inversion of stitches in knitting to produce a ribbed effect" ("Purl"^{2} [vt.], def 3). Thus, the weaver of the *tesseract* is either Clotho, in Greek and Roman mythology "that one of the three Fates who spins the thread of human life" ("Clotho" [n.], def.), or the narrator himself. *Bootstrap*

Their eyes like wheels: Here, android eyes evoke "the inter-revolving wheels that 'were full of eyes round about,'" the God-image in Ezekiel 1.18 (Jung, *Mysterium Coniunctionis* 207). Jung adds that, since "Eyes are round and in common speech are likened to 'cart-wheels,'" they also appear to be "a typical symbol for what I have called the 'multiple luminosities of the unconscious.'" *Ephesian Symbols*

They wash Him then rinse, sprinkle then immerse: the death of Christ on the Cross construed as a rite of passage, a change of role and status. See *The Body in Question,* where Jonathan Miller explains that "The idea of 'rites of passage' was first introduced by the French anthropologist Arnold Van Gennep in 1909. Van Gennep insisted that all rituals of 'passing through' occurred in three successive phases: a rite of separation, a rite of transition and a rite of aggregation. The person whose status is to be changed has to undergo a ritual which marks his departure from the old version of himself: there has to be some act which symbolizes the fact that he has rid himself of all his previous associations. He is washed, rinsed, sprinkled or immersed, and, in this way, all his previous obligations and attachments are symbolically untied and even annihilated. This stage is followed by a rite of transition, when the person is neither fish nor fowl; he has left his old status behind him but has not yet assumed his new one. This liminal condition is usually marked by rituals of isolation and segregation—a period of vigil, mockery perhaps, fear and trembling. There are often elaborate rites of humiliation—scourging, insults, and darkness. Finally, in the rite of aggregation, the new status is ritually conferred: the person is admitted, enrolled, confirmed and ordained" (51-52). *Spacetime's Wight*

Thinsulate: here, a synthetic thermal-insulation fiber used in the wayfinder's clothing. *The Cusp of Skill*

those Forms in caves: In The Allegory of the Cave, from Book VII of *The Republic,* Plato demonstrates the difference between the material things that we perceive in the world—objects likened by Plato to shadows projected upon a cave wall—and the archetypal Forms from which they derive their fundamental reality. *Storyboard*

A thousand gemstones on Möbius' run: the climax of the speaker's numinous dream life. See Chevalier and Gheerbrant, *The Penguin Dictionary of Symbols* 939: "Precious stones are the symbol of the transmutation of the opaque into the translucent and, in a spiritual sense, of darkness into light and imperfection into perfection. Thus the Heavenly Jerusalem is completely encrusted in precious stones. [. . .] This means that in this new universe all states and levels of existence will have undergone a radical transformation in the direction of a perfection unequalled in this world and characterized by spirituality and luminosity." *Cat's Eye*

thumb: The speaker alludes to the mysterious thumbling, a creative dwarf (not unlike Tom Thumb) who is a personification of "the hidden [or subterranean] forces of nature" (Jung, *The Archetypes and the Collective Unconscious* 158). *Storyboard; The Water That Does Not Make the Hands Wet*

Till darkness descends, impartial or shy, / *Even as the lid of a closing eye:* Cf. Mark Vanhoenacker, "At the Solstice, in Praise of Darkness," *The New York Times* 16 Dec. 2017: 1 <www.nytimes.com/2017/12/16/opinion/sunday/solstice-praise-for-darkness.html>: "For the roughly 90 percent of us who live in the Northern Hemisphere, the winter solstice of 2017 is coming soon (at 11:28 a.m. E.S.T. on Thursday, to be precise). [. . .] the year's longest night is sweeping down over the northern half of our [tilted] planet, as naturally as the lid of a closing eye." *Gatekeeper*

till Saturn's boons— / Like alphabet rings and habitable moons— / With Jupiter reckon in Castor's runes: The speaker updates an ongoing cosmic contest: "Twenty new moons have been found around Saturn, giving the ringed planet a total of 82 [. . .]. That beats Jupiter and its 79 moons." See Marcia Dunn, "New 'moon king': Saturn passes Jupiter with 20-moon discovery," *The Christian Science Monitor* 8 Oct. 2019: 1-2 <www.csmonitor.com>. In these lines, Castor, one of the twin sons of Zeus, becomes the surrogate astronaut who crafts "mystical or obscure" poems or songs ("Rune" [n.], def. 3b)— even about Saturn's *boons* or blessings. See the note on *Like alphabet rings* given above. *Rite*

till the world-egg crack: The *world-egg* is "the philosophical egg of the medieval natural philosophers, the vessel from which, at the end of the *opus alchymicum,* the homunculus emerges, that is, the Anthropos, the spiritual, inner, and complete man [. . .]" (Jung, *The Archetypes and the Collective Unconscious* 293). *The Heavenly Journey of the Shaman*

Tipler's subset: a variant of the Everett-Dewitt or many-universes interpretation of quantum mechanics. See Davies, *The Mind of God* 126: Frank J. Tipler, a professor of Mathematical Physics at Tulane University, "believes that all possible universes that can support consciousness [are] experienced" and that "The set of programs capable of generating cognizable [i.e., knowable] universes will be a small subset of the set of all possible programs." Our *subset* "can be regarded as typical." *Fabricator*

To each and all it is given to dance: an excerpt from The Acts of John in the New Testament apocrypha, "a description of a mystical 'round dance' which Christ instituted before his crucifixion. He told his disciples to hold hands and form a ring, while he himself stood in the centre. As they moved round in a circle, Christ sang a song of praise," quoted here in the following "characteristic" verses: "'The Twelve paces the round aloft, Amen. / To each and all it is given to dance, Amen'" (Jung, *Psychology and Western Religion* 169-70). *The Round Dance of the Stars*

to his surprise, / The biped, though he dies, increase his size: In the speaker's view, the "big bounce" model of the universe is an unexpected analogue to "What the Father has purposed, and the Son has [either] procured" [or, rather, *purchased*] for us (Murray, *The Spirit of Christ* 167)—the Biblical promise of life after death. See John 11.25-26: "Jesus said, 'I am the resurrection and I am life. If a man has faith in me, even though he die[s], he shall come to life; and no one who is alive and has faith shall ever die.'" *Splitting the Earth with a Straight Foot*

To Paradox and Mystery we cling: In this "impulsive," "ecstatic," "cosmic" stanza, *paradoxically*, as each dancer clasps the hand of the Messiah, "knowing" becomes a *personal* act of tacit *integration* and [unlike the structure of the lyric itself construed as the poet's *formal* statement] in no way resembles "an impersonal achievement of detached objectivity [. . .] grounded on explicit operations of logic" (Michael Polyani and Harry Prosch, *Meaning* [Chicago: The U of Chicago P, 1975] 63). See also Jung's useful assessment in *Psychology* *and Western Religion* 171: "Paradox is a characteristic of the Gnostic writings. It does more justice to the unknowable than clarity can do, for uniformity of meaning robs the mystery of its darkness and sets it up as something that is *known*. That is a usurpation, and it leads the human intellect into hybris by pretending that it, the intellect, has got hold of the transcendent mystery by a cognitive act and has grasped it. The paradox therefore reflects a higher level of intellect and, by not forcibly representing the unknowable as known, gives a more faithful picture of the real state of affairs." *The Round Dance of the Stars*

torus: the universe pictured as a hyperdoughnut, one of the "strange topologies" that Michio Kaku predicates in *Hyperspace* 94-98. *Cosmic Dust*

transcendent as jade: See Chevalier and Gheerbrant, *The Penguin Dictionary of Symbols* 549: "Its beauty makes jade an emblem of perfection; of the five transcendent qualities of benignity, lucidity, resonance, immutability and purity; of most of the moral virtues of charity, prudence, justice, grace, harmony, sincerity and good faith; as well as of Heaven and Earth, of righteousness and [. . .] 'the way of righteousness.'" *A Host-Star in Draco*

the Tree on the knoll: the cross to which the dying Jesus was fastened ouitside Jerusalem on a small hill called Golgotha, "which means 'Place of a skull'" (Matt. 27.33). *A Methane Snow*

tubers that fill: In "How Pottery Offers Glimpses Into Ancient Foodways," Carolyn Wilke reports that, during the Bronze and Iron Ages, "Ceramic vessels helped change what people ate—they could boil meat for stews, for example, or cook [stem] tubers [like potatoes, artichokes, turnips, and yams] long enough to destroy toxins" (*Sapiens* 8 Sept. 2021: 5 <www.sapiens.org>). *The Cusp of Skill*

tuning fork: "a small steel instrument with two prongs, which when struck sounds a certain fixed tone in perfect pitch; it is used as a guide in tuning instruments, in testing hearing, etc." ("Tuning-fork" [def.]), and, here, in tracking wave-energy vibrational fields cognized from the biocentric universe and from the human body. *Psalter*

Twin of two natures: In the Cabalistic view, "Man and his heavenly prototype are 'twins'" (Jung, *Mysterium Coniunctionis* 413n198). *Trapeze*

A unicorn that sprints: "a mythical horselike animal with a single horn growing from the center of its forehead" ("Unicorn" [n.], def. 1). Jung notes that "the symbol of the unicorn as an allegory of Christ and of the Holy Ghost was current all through the Middle Ages" (*Psychology and Alchemy* 438). On the same page, see also fig. 241: "Virgin taming a [sprinting] unicorn." *Spacetime's Wight*

vas: See Jung, *Psychology and Alchemy* 236n15: The Hermetic vessel is "a circular instrument, a [well-sealed] phial of spherical shape." *Light of the Eye*

Venusian as jade: In this poem, *jade*—the androgynous royal gem of China symbolic of wisdom, courage, compassion, and beauty—is also *Venusian* because of still another of its sacred properties: "the concentrated essence of love." *A Host-Star in Draco*

Venusian as the moon: In even remote mythologies, Venus "was the Moon's daughter and the Sun's sister and, since she appeared at dawn and [at] dusk, it was only natural that she should be regarded as some sort of link between the deities of light and darkness" (Chevalier and Gheerbrant, *The Penguin Dictionary of Symbols* 1064). *The Heavenly Journey of the Shaman*

Venus in the dunes / Transits into twilight till Saturn's boons— / [. . .] With Jupiter reckon in Castor's runes: The speaker recalls the Cassini-Huygens space-research mission, which lasted for almost twenty years, from 15 October 1997 to 15 September 2017. See Jay R. Thompson, "Scenic Route to Saturn," *NASA Solar System Exploration* 8 June 2017: 1 <https://solarsystem.nasa.gov/news>: Cassini's interplanetary route began with a launch from Earth, "followed by gravity-assist flybys of Venus, Earth, and Jupiter. During each flyby, orbital momentum was transferred from each planet to the spacecraft, increasing the spacecraft's velocity relative to the sun so [that] Cassini could reach [its main objective] Saturn." Here, Castor, one of the twins of Zeus, is also the speaker's surrogate astronaut who crafts "mystical or obscure" poems or songs ("Rune" [n.], def. 3b). See also the note on *Like alphabet rings* given above. *Rite*

volcanoes that we know, / Salmon-tinted Pluto, a methane snow: See "50 Greatest Moments of the Space Age," *Air&Space Smithsonian: Collector's Edition* (Summer 2017): The NASA-approved New Horizons mission, launched in 2006, "zipped past Pluto in July 2015. The salmon-tinted world turned out to be far more interesting and diverse than scientists had predicted, with possible ice volcanoes, methane snow, and a surprising amount of geological activity for such a cold planet" (89). *A Methane Snow*

wain: a cart or a large, open farm wagon—here, an emblem of lowly social status. *Gateway*

walks without a cleat: Shuttle spacewalkers wore outer boots that "did not need to be as flexible as those used on the Moon's surface or [. . .] inside the craft." Instead, the shoe featured a "rigid sole" with a fitted clip that "could locate and secure into foot restraints on the exterior of the ISS [the International Space Station] and on the robotic arm" (Stuart Morgan, "Footwear in the extreme environment of space," *SATRA Bulletin* May 2010, *SATRA Technology* 1 Nov. 2014: 4 <www.satra.co.uk.bulletin>). *The Man in the Moon*

Wash me, and I shall be whiter than snow: an excerpt from Psalm 51, verse 7, in the Old Testament, a poem that, according to Jung, focuses on the black Shulamite and the reborn Adam. Thus, in *Mysterium Coniunctionis,* Jung explains that, in alchemical literature, the black Shulamite, the priestess of Ishtar, "signifies earth, nature, fertility, everything that flourishes under the damp light of the moon, and also the natural life-urge." In effect, the Shulamite personifies "the original man [Adam] in his savage, unredeemed state." Nevertheless, the "subject of transformation is not the empirical man, however much he may identify with the 'old Adam,' but Adam the Primordial Man, the archetype within us"—i.e., "the still older Adam before the Fall, Adam Kadmon." Apparently "the coming to consciousness of Adam Kadmon would indeed be a great illumination, for it would be a realization of the inner man or Anthropos, an archetypal totality transcending the sexes." In fact, the "Shulamite's hope of becoming a 'white dove' points to a future, perfect state. The white dove is a hint that the Shulamite will become Sophia, the Holy Ghost, while Adam Kadmon is an obvious parallel of Christ" (452-54). *The Smoke-Hole of the Tent*

water *is* fire: According to the alchemists, "the concepts of water, fire, and spirit coalesce as they do in religious usage." Thus, "according to the hymn of St. Romanus on the theophany [the direct, albeit temporary, manifestation of God in sensible form], He "who was seen of old in the midst of three children as dew in the fire, [was] now a fire flickering and shining in the Jordan, himself the light inaccessible'" (Jung, *Alchemical Studies* 74n31). *The Moon in Transition Raised to the Sun*

The water that does not make the hands wet: In alchemy, "Quicksilver, because of its fluidity and volatility," was often "defined as water." Thus, a popular saying was "'Aqua manus non madefaciens' (the water that does not make the hands wet)." In fact, in order to emphasize the "sublimated" nature of the "philosophic" Mercurius, many treatises refer to him as *water* (Jung, *Alchemical Studies* 207). *The Water That Does Not Make the Hands Wet*

a wave through a sieve: i.e., a probability wave. See the notes on *A quantum of light* and *qwiff* given above. *Schrödinger's Cat*

Waxing in Luna into the Nature of the Sun: In the alchemical *opus,* "the arcane substance, whether in neuter or personified form, rises from the earth, unites the opposites, and then returns to earth, thereby achieving its own transformation into the elixir [of life]" (Jung, *Mysterium Coniunctionis* 219). Thus, in the "Consilium coniungii" (*Ars chemica* [1566]), the soul rises up from the [procreative] sulphur "and is exalted to the heavens, that is, to the spirit, and becomes the rising sun (that is, red), in the waxing moon, and of solar nature." Jung notes that the latter phrase—in the original Latin, "In Luna crescente, in naturam solarem"—"could also be translated: 'waxing in Luna into the nature of the sun'" (220n546). *Waxing in Luna into the Nature of the Sun*

We assemble the station: i.e., the International Space Station (ISS), a habitable artificial satellite launched into low-Earth orbit in 1998. *The Smoke-Hole of the Tent*

We become a child and a fish at once: See Jung, *Symbols of Transformation* 198: "The fish in dreams occasionally signifies the unborn child, because the child before its birth lives in the water like a fish"; within weeks, during its fetal phase, "becomes child and fish at once"; and, like the astrological Christ, the first *fish* of the Pisces era, "is therefore a symbol of renewal and rebirth." *Rebis*

We board NASA's capsule; like Hermes curl; / Capture an asteroid: See Erin Mahoney, "How Will NASA's Asteroid Redirect Mission Help Humans Reach Mars?" NASA 27 June 2014: 1 <nasa.gov>: "NASA is developing the first ever [robotic] mission to identify, capture and relocate an asteroid to a stable orbit around the moon, and send [human] astronauts to return samples of it to Earth. This Asteroid Redirect Mission (ARM) will greatly advance NASA's human path to Mars, testing the capabilities needed for future crewed missions to the Red Planet." Last updated 7 Aug. 2017. See also the note on *Gateway* given above. *The Smoke-Hole of the Tent*

  We can trace its path; through Ge's eyepiece glean— / [. . .] Zodiacal light in capsules of sheen: the faint, ever-shifting "illumination [of the 13 constellations of the Zodiac] along the ecliptic [the apparent path of the sun during the course of a year], visible in the west just after sunset and in the east just before sunrise" ("Zodiacal Light," def.). *Cosmic Dust*

  We collapse the wave: See the note on *qwiff* given above. *The Spear of Archytas*

  We edit His skein like a rumored pain: As the avowed temple of the Holy Spirit (1 Cor. 6.19), each indwelt believer can identify with the Savior's agony on the Cross through "fellowship with God" (Murray, *The Spirit of Christ* 217), the "habit" of a Christian life (37). Cf. also Miller, *The Body in Question* 44-45: "The experience of friends and neighbors [. . .] plays a large part in the editing of sensations. If someone we know has heart trouble, it is only too easy to reshape our own sensations until they come to resemble his. Most of us have scattered pains in and around the chest at some time or another, and, unless we are abnormally sensitive, we disregard them. But if one of our friends or relatives is known to have something wrong with his heart, these scattered sensations grow together and easily assume the shape and permanence of the rumoured pain." Here, *skein* is both narrative thread and the coil of life. *Spacetime's Wight*

  We enter the retort: In this clause, the term *retort* signifies both the Hermetic vessel and a sleight-of-hand pun—in effect, a jubilant reply to the question in the preceding line: "What shall we say—that Chaos is first?" The answer is, simply enough, that "humans are woven into the entire cosmic network" (Margaret Wertheim, "God Is Also a Cosmologist," *The New York Times* 8 June 1997: 4 <www.nytimes.com>); that God "upholds the [holistic] universe by the word of His power" (Heb. 1.3); and that, as a result, *The Omniverse itself [is] predestinate* (line 16), i.e., foreordained (Acts 4.28) and purposeful (Eph. 1.11). See the note on *Heaven's mate— / Ge's coheir—implicate* given above. *Local Bubble*

  We enter the subset as through a door: In *The Physics of Immortality: Modern Cosmology, God and the Resurrection of the Dead* (New York: Doubleday, 1994), Frank J. Tipler argues that a "person" is "a computer program that can pass the Turing test" (210)—i.e., can behave in every way like a person. However, Tipler adds that, as "an entity that codes information," each of us may be but a "subsimulation"—in effect, a simulation "embedded inside a larger simulation that does not stop" (211). In fact, Tipler also suggests that "a person is not resurrected until he or she is emulated; that is, duplicated down to the exact quantum state" (225). *Chain-Linked*

  We fasten His tunic without a seam: The speaker refers to the "visible seam or suture" with which the opposites (e.g., male/female; light/darkness; consciousness/unconsciousness) are united, as in the archetype of the androgynous Original Man, an alchemical symbol of the self. By contrast, in the higher Adam, "the opposition is invisible" (Jung, *Aion* 248). *The Woman in the Moon*

We have trampled on the garment of shame: See "the fragment from the Gospel according to the Egyptians cited [by the Greek Christian theologian] Clement of Alexandria" (c. 150 - c. 215) and quoted by C. G. Jung in *Mysterium Coniunctionis* 374: "'When ye have trampled on the garment of shame, and when the two become one and the male with the female is neither male nor female.'" *Courtship*

We journey in the vessel of the Sun: The NASA astronaut—like Hercules, an evolving god-man—advances into the unknown regions of both Spacetime and the psyche. According to Jung, symbolically, Hercules, the Greek sun-hero, descended into "the dark world of the unconscious," even as he undertook "the perilous adventure of the night sea journey, [. . .] whose end and aim is the restoration of life, resurrection, and the triumph over death" (*Psychology and Alchemy* 329). See also 334, fig. 171: "Hercules on the night sea journey in the vessel of the sun," a design on the "Base of an Attic vase (5th cent. B.C.)." *Claim*

We network Ge's android; [. . .] bi-ocular, bond: The speaker refers to the Helmet Mounted Display (HMD)—here, an optical system with one objective lens and two eyepieces for simultaneous observation by both eyes—that NASA's telepresent operator uses in order to immerse himself visually in the dexterous humanoid robot's workplace. See Joe Bibby and Ryan Necessary, "Telepresence," *Robonaut 1* <robonaut.jsc.nasa.gov>. Last updated 13 Mar. 2008. *Evangelist*

We platform the station, gateway to the stars: See Kelli Mars, "Gateway," NASA 27 June 2022: 1<nasa.gov>: "Gateway will be humanity's first space station in lunar orbit to support deep space exploration plans, along with the Space Launch System (SLS) rocket, the Orion spacecraft, and the Human Landing System (HLS) that will send astronauts to the Moon." See also the note on *Gateway* given above. *The Smoke-Hole of the Tent*

We pre-breathe in the airlock: on board a shuttle orbiter, *the airlock* is "an [airtight] cylindrical chamber located at the end of the mid-deck," where astronauts don their spacesuits (Herrod, *Space Walks* 46) and then *pre-breathe* pure oxygen for a few hours in order to rid themselves of the nitrogen in their bodies that can cause gas bubbles and "bending" when they leave the orbiting station. *The Moon in Transition Raised to the Sun*

We search such a world as the Sun devised: / An acidic soup, its spores fossilized, / Then found in space rocks: In the highly mobilized quest for the origins of life, Richard Hoover, a NASA scientist, reports that he has detected "tiny fossilized bacteria on three meteorites," even as he argues that "these microscopic life forms are not native to Earth. If confirmed, this research would suggest [that] life in the universe is widespread and [that] life on Earth may have come from elsewhere in the solar system" and may have traveled to our planet "on space rocks like comets, moons, and other astral bodies." See Deborah Zabarenko,

"Strange life signs found on meteorites: NASA scientist," REUTERS 16 Nov. 2021: 1-2 <www.reuters.com>. *Gateway*

We shoulder our way, the air like a hiss: Here, the speaker evokes an "alchemystical" symbol of the "aerial soul" (Jung, *Psychology and Alchemy* 237n7). Thus, since "all things are imagined or pictured in air through the power of fire" (282), the archetypal astronaut, like both writer and reader, "climbs from the launch pad on a pillar of smoke and flame" (Robin Kerrod, *Space Walks* [New York: Gallery-Smith, 1985] 43), even as, seconds after lift-off, he enters the "subtle reality" that exists between mind and matter (Jung 283). In this context, the *air* is at once wind, atmosphere, sky, space above the earth, and, not least of all, melody: an arrangement of sounds in sequence. *Psalter*

We slumber in matter: In the teachings of Basilides, an early Christian Gnostic, "Just as the man Jesus became conscious only through the light that emanated from the higher Christ and separated the natures in him, so the seed in unconscious humanity is awakened by the light emanating from Jesus, and is thereby impelled to a similar discrimination of opposites" (Jung, *Aion* 67). *Psalter*

We try each door that the Hubble unlocked: In "When Galaxies Collide," Begley ponders "all the secrets that the Hubble [Space Telescope] has unlocked," especially "its images of galaxies that formed when the universe was in its infancy" (5). *Courtship*

We watch through each eye His particle wave: According to the quantum theory of matter, the atom will not emit "just any amount of light, but pulses or packets that contain a given quantity of energy, characteristic for each type of atom" (Davies, *Other Worlds* 32), and that function as both "wave of probability" (64) and *particle*. However, Davies emphasizes that, although "Chaos lies at the heart of matter," and that "random changes, restrained only by probabilistic laws, endow the fabric of the universe with a roulette-like quality" (92), the "act of experience requires two components: the observer and the observed." In fact, "It is the mutual interaction between them that supplies our sensations of a surrounding 'reality'" (108). In effect, the *active* sentient observer, entwining the light, collapses the *wave* of probability into reality. *Waxing in Luna into the Nature of the Sun*

What now I am seen to be I am not: a declaration of divine unity that Jesus voices in the Acts of John and that Jung interprets in *Psychology and Western Religion*. In other words, through his union with Christ, the speaker mirrors the Savior not only as an "empirical man," but also as "a (transcendental) whole" (176-77). For further clarification of this verse, see the note on *I will be united* given above. *Scintilla's Scan*

what Zacchaeus heard: See Luke 19.1-10: In Jericho, "There was a man there named Zacchaeus; he was superintendent of taxes and very rich. He was eager to see what Jesus looked like; but, being a little man, he could not see him for the crowd. So he ran on ahead and climbed a sycomore-tree in order to see him, for he was to pass that way. When Jesus came to the place, he looked up and said, 'Zacchaeus, be quick and come down; I must come and stay with you today.' He climbed down as fast as he could and welcomed him gladly. At this there was a general murmur of disapproval. 'He has gone in,' they said, 'to be the guest of a sinner.' But Zacchaeus stood there and said to the Lord, 'Here and now, sir, I give half my possessions to charity; and if I have cheated anyone, I am ready to repay him four times over.' Jesus said to him, 'Salvation has come to this house today!—for this man too is a son of Abraham, and the Son of Man has come to seek and save what is lost.''' In effect, as the Flemish mystic John of Ruysbroeck (1294-1381) notes in *The Adornment of the Spiritual Marriage*, Zacchaeus "'must climb up into the tree of faith, which grows from above downwards,'" because "'its roots are in the Godhead'" (qtd. in Jung, *Mysterium Coniunctionis* 135n210). *The Jesus of Psychoanalysis*

wheel: See Chevalier and Gheerbrant, *The Penguin Dictionary of Symbols:* In the majority of cultures, the *wheel* "is a solar symbol," even as the Sun itself is either "a god or a manifestation of the godhead" (945). *Scion*

When Adam scattered skein [. . .] / Yahweh ran His fane: a mind-twisting synopsis of Redemption's narrative thread: the Fall of Adam and Eve (Gen. 3.1-24); the Binding of Isaac (Gen. 22.1-18); the Translation of Elijah (2 Kings 2.1-18); the Birth, Resurrection, and Ascension of Christ (Luke 2.1-20; John 11.25-26), and the Savior's Millennial Return (Rev. 20.1-7). *Here Be Dragons*

When old stars in globular clusters merge, / Out of their ashes protoplanets surge: Cf. Begley, "When Galaxies Collide" 4: "In the ultimate heavenly recycling, old stars in globular clusters merge, and out of their ashes [or gas] a new star is born. Contrary to the textbooks, globular clusters do not contain only old stars." *Courtship*

Who knows how it was, and who shall declare / That Creation is rare, and who shall care / That bodies dissemble that Spirits wear / Or metaverses tear in Saturn's lair?: a roundabout validation of Jung's thesis that "the God-image is immediately related to, or identical with, the self" (Jung, *Aion* 109). Thus, "The idea that the world-creating Deity is not conscious, but may be dreaming, is found even in the Old Testament, not to speak of the New," and also in Hindu literature—for example, in the *Rig-Veda* [X, 129], which Jung references in *Aion* 192: "'Who knows how it was, and who shall declare / Whence it was born and whence it came? [. . .] He alone who sees all in the highest heaven / Knows—or does not know.'" In other words, "As the Godhead is essentially unconscious, so too is the man who lives in God." In fact, Meister Eckhart, the thirteenth-century Christian Neoplatonist, counsels the mystic seeker to "love God in the following way: 'Love him as he is: a not-God, a not-spirit, a not-person, a not-image; as a sheer, pure, clear One, which he is, sundered from all secondness; and in this one let us sink eternally from nothing to nothing. So help us God. Amen'" (*Works,* trans. C. de B. Evans, vol. 1 [London, 1924] 247-48; qtd. in Jung, *Aion* 193). *Claim*

wholeness His aim / *From below upwards:* For the Naassenes, the ithyphallic Hermes Kyllenios (both a synonym for Christ as second Adam and a Gnostic symbol of the self) is "'the Logos, the interpreter and fashioner of what has been, is, and will be.' That is why he is worshipped as the phallus, because he, like the male organ, 'has an urge [. . .] from below upwards'" (Jung, *Aion* 201-02). *Extract of the Macrocosm*

wight: "a living being; [a] creature" ("Wight[1]" [n.], def. 1). *Fixated on Mars; Spacetime's Wight*

Windmill: "either a mill operated by the wind's rotation of large, oblique sails or vanes radiating from a shaft" ("Windmill" [n.], def. 1), or "anything like a windmill, as a propeller-like toy," a *pinwheel,* "revolved by [the] wind" (def. 2). See also Jung, *Psychology and Alchemy* 307, fig. 158, "The Mill of the Host," where "The Word, in the form of scrolls, is poured into a mill by the four evangelists, to reappear as the Infant Christ in the chalice." *Scion*

With a Cup, / Conquered Time and Mephistopheles' pup: Through the sacrament of the Holy Eucharist—"the sign that *we belong to God,* that we are *His possession,* His chosen ones," even as "He comes to us and gives Himself to us as *our* possession" (Merton, *The Living Bread* 113)—Christ has overcome both Time and the Devil, the demon here represented by Mephistopheles, who, in Christopher Marlowe's *Doctor Faustus* (1588), Act 3, Scene 3, turns Robin, Faustus' servant, into a dog. In the poem, at this point, the faith-centered speaker is perhaps also self-mocking, because—as Merton suggests—"The higher we rise in the religious scale, and the more spiritual our notion of God becomes, the more we realize the infinite distance between Him and ourselves." Of course, "at the same time we cannot escape the realization of His all-pervading immanence" (56). *The Jesus of Psychoanalysis*

With a straight foot the foetus splits the ground: See the note on *Sown from the ash, the mother of lances* given above. *Splitting the Earth with a Straight Foot*

With but a codicil and then a plea: According to the speaker, in addition to the gifts of salvation and resurrection that Christ has bequeathed to the faithful, He has added a *codicil,* i.e., a certain provision, to His will, along with an urgent entreaty. See Matt. 6.33-34: "'Set your mind on God's kingdom and his justice before everything else, and all the rest will come to you as well. So do not be anxious about tomorrow; tomorrow will look after itself.'" *Scintilla's Scan*

with heat that chars, / The breath of the Spirit: See Jung, *Symbols of Transformation* 317n19: "In the Mithraic liturgy, the generating breath of the spirit comes from the sun." Mithras was an ancient Persian sun-god. *Splitting the Earth with a Straight Foot*

With His consummate eye: a pun that emphasizes the "complete or perfect" vision of the Messiah ("Consummate" [adj.], def. 1) even as it recalls His dying words on the Cross—"Consummatus est": "It is accomplished" ("Consummate" [vt.], def. 1). *Scintilla's Scan*

with Horus-eyes Bes: In ancient Egyptian mythology, *Bes,* a bearded, dwarfish god, is the protector of mothers, children, childbirth, and households. His "feminine aspect" (and female counterpart) is Beset. *Horus* is the falcon-headed Egyptian sky god, the son of Isis and Osiris. His right eye represented the sun; his left eye, the moon. See Joshua J. Mark,

"Bes," *Ancient History Encyclopedia* 7 Nov. 2016: 1 <www.ancient.eu/Bes/>, and also Jung, *Symbols of Transformation* 213, fig. 11: "Bes, with Horus-eyes," the latter image representing the cosmic battle between light and darkness. *The Woman in the Moon*

 With inch-worming arm and two-fingered hand, / [. . .] / Unhook attached components: details from NASA's view, now retrospective, of the piece-by-piece assembly of the 1-million pound International Space Station: Humankind "has begun a move off of the planet Earth of unprecedented scale. Astronauts will perform more spacewalks in the next [ten] years than have been conducted since space flight began, more than two and a half times as many. They will be assisted by an 'inch-worming' robotic arm; a two-fingered 'Canada hand'; and maybe even a free-flying robotic 'eye' that can circle and inspect the station" ("International Space Station Assembly: A Construction Site in Orbit," *NASA Facts* June 1999: 1 <https://er.jsc.nasa.gov>). *The Moon in Transition Raised to the Sun*

 without a seam: The speaker refers to the visible *seam* or suture with which the opposites (e.g., light/darkness; consciousness/unconsciousness) are united, as in the symbol of the *rebis*. By contrast, in the higher Adam, "the opposition is invisible" (Jung, *Aion* 248). *The Woman in the Moon*

 Without a shadow, its surface colder: In search of "a level landing area" on the Moon for the crew of Apollo 11, "NASA's mission planners had given plenty of forethought to the photometrics involved. They had concluded that, for optimum depth perception, *Eagle* needed to land at a time of 'day' and at an angle that produced the longest possible shadows. Where there were no shadows, the Moon looked flat, but where shadows were long, the Moon looked fully three-dimensional. An astronaut could then perceive depth on the lunar surface very well: he could detect differences in elevation; he could easily identify the accented shapes and forms of peaks, valleys, craters, ridges, and rims. The ideal condition occurred for the trajectory of the L[unar] M[odule] when the Sun was 12.5 degrees above the horizon. That was the time when Armstrong and Aldrin would have adequate light over the area and still strong depth-of-field definition [. . .]" (Hansen, *First Man* 467). In other words, "Seeing the LM's shadow was helpful because it was an added visual cue of how high they were" (469). *Waxing in Luna into the Nature of the Sun*

 Without rust I waken: the speaker's piercing self-evaluation. See Jung, *Psychology and Alchemy* 159: "In the alchemical view rust, like verdigris [its green, or greenish-blue, coating], is the metal's sickness. But at the same time this leprosy is [. . .] the basis for the preparation of the philosophical gold." Thus, "The paradoxical remark of Thales [c. 624 BC– c. 546 BC] that the rust alone gives the coin its true value is a kind of alchemical quip, which at bottom only says that there is no light without shadow and no psychic wholeness without imperfection. To round itself out, life calls not for perfection but for completeness; and for this the 'thorn in the flesh' is needed, the suffering of defects without which there is no progress and no ascent." *Splitting the Earth with a Straight Foot*

 Woman and dragon embrace in the grave: In alchemy, "woman appears as the true carrier of the longed-for wholeness and redemption" (Jung, *Mysterium Coniunctionis* 357), while the dragon "is the chthonic forerunner of the self" (224). However, elsewhere, Jung explains that, before the artifex achieves the goal of the *opus*—resuscitation, transfiguration, and the "indescribable totality" of the self (155)—"The soul as Luna attains its plenilunium, its sunlike brilliance, [but] then wanes into the novilunium and sinks down into the embrace of the terrestrial sulphur, which here signifies death and corruption." In fact, "We are reminded of the gruesome conjunction at the new moon in Maier's *Scrutinium chymicum*, where the woman and the dragon embrace in the grave" (220). *Waxing in Luna into the Nature of the Sun*

Worlds lit by auroras: See Moore, *Travellers in Space and Time* 54: "Next we pass over Jupiter's night hemisphere, the side turned away from the Sun. A brilliant display of aurorae stretches for thousands of miles, basically similar in nature to the aurorae or polar lights that we see from high latitudes on Earth and which are caused by electrified particles entering the upper atmosphere. The particles causing our aurorae are due to the active volcanoes on Io [one of Jupiter's many moons]. Over the night side there are lightning flashes, and if we could venture outside our spaceship we would hear incessant thunder. Jupiter is a noisy planet as well as a brilliant one, at least at some wavelengths." *A Host-Star in Draco*

The world that we weave is as strange as waves: The speaker means that, in the quantum description of matter, the wave-like aspect of elementary particles is but "a spread of probability" (Davies, *Other Worlds* 63). *Storyboard*

the world-wheel yet turns: not only Ezekiel's mobile *world-wheel,* a quaternary symbol for the Spirit of Life that moved "like a wheel inside a wheel" (Ezek. 1.17-18), but also, in holistic Dynamic cosmology, "Space [. . .] defined as the three-dimensional surface of a four-dimensional sphere free to contract and expand in an infinite four-dimensional universe." See Tiomola Suntola, *The Dynamic Universe: Toward a Unified Picture of Physical Reality,* 4th ed. (2011; Finland: Physics Foundations Society and The Finnish Society for Natural Philosophy, 2018) 284 <www.protsv.fi>. Web. 19 Sept. 2020. *Fabricator*

Yod: both the tenth letter of the Hebrew alphabet and the Gnostic symbol of the indivisible point, i.e., of the "perfect and indivisible man." Thus, "The Original Man, Adam, signifies the small hook at the top of the letter Yod [']" (Jung, *Aion* 218n136). The word rhymes with "wood." *The Smoke-Hole of the Tent; The Water That Does Not Make the Hands Wet*

Your cloudform ferried from another state, / I sift you that I may fulfill my fate: The speaker emphasizes that, during the Communion rite, "Christian devotion never in practice separates the accidents of bread from the substance of Christ under the sacramental species." In effect, "the Blessed Eucharist" comes to us "as the food of our souls" (Merton, *The Living Bread* 83), even as each communicant, "the perishable, conscious individual" (Jung, *Psychology and Alchemy* 10), triumphs over and above "the ephemeral and 'accidental' mortal man" (48). *The Chariot of Aristotle's Wheels*

Zion's cenacle: in the Holy Bible, the Room of the Last Supper, construed here as the originary site of "that new Jerusalem which is coming down out of heaven" after End-time and the second creation of Heaven and Earth (Rev. 3.12). *Trapeze*

www.ingramcontent.com/pod-product-compliance
Lightning Source LLC
Chambersburg PA
CBHW051357110526
44592CB00023B/2859